the earliest christian
HYMNBOOK

the earliest christian
HYMNBOOK

The Odes of Solomon

TRANSLATED BY

James H. Charlesworth

CASCADE *Books* · Eugene, Oregon

THE FIRST CHRISTIAN HYMNBOOK
The Odes of Solomon

Cascade Books
A Division of Wipf and Stock Publishers
199 W. 8th Ave., Suite 3
Eugene, OR 97401

www.wipfandstock.com

ISBN 13: 978-1-60608-646-9

Cataloging-in-Publication data:

The first Christian hymnbook : the Odes of Solomon / Translated
by James H. Charlesworth.

ISBN 13: 978-1-60608-646-9

xxxviii + 134 p. ; 23 cm. Includes bibliographic references
and index.

1. Odes of Solomon—Translation. 2. Christian poetry, Early.
I. Charlesworth, James H. II. Title.

BS1830 O3 S9 2009

Manufactured in the U.S.A.

Cover illustration is a registered trademark by
"The Odes Project" 2008, used by permission.

This book is dedicated to:

my children and grandchildren
Michelle, Eve, James, Isabelle, and Jack James

and
my admired colleagues in Princeton

as well as
Jim Joyner, John Hoffmann, and Dan Hales,
Officers in the Foundation on Judaism and Christian
Origins

CONTENTS

ABBREVIATIONS

1Q	The abbreviation for manuscripts from Qumran Cave 1
1QH^a	*Thanksgiving Hymns^a* (*Hodayot*)
1QM	*War Scroll* (*Milḥamah*),
1QS	*Rule of the Community* (*Serek ha-Yaḥad*)
1QSb	*Blessings* (Appendix to 1QS)
1Q27	*Book of the Mysteries*
5ApocSyrPss	*5 Apocryphal Syriac Psalms*
C	Coptic Manuscript of five *Odes*, known as Codex Askewianus, located in the British Museum, London
CD	*Damascus Document*
G	Greek Manuscript of *Ode* 11 in Bodmer Papyrus XI
H	Syriac Manuscript H (Harris) of the *Odes*, located in the John Rylands Library, Manchester, England
N	Syriac Manuscript N (Nitriensis) of the *Odes*, located in the British Museum, London

More than any Evangelist, the author of the Fourth Gospel emphasizes Jesus' hope that his followers will have "joy." In the Farewell Discourses, or "the Testament of Jesus," Jesus is reported to state: "These (words) I have spoken to you, that my joy may be in you, and that your joy may be full" (John 15:1).

Jesus is portrayed as seeing the suffering of his followers; but he predicts they will finally experience joy. Notice how this joy is expressed poetically:

> Truly, truly, I say to you, you will weep and lament,
> But the world will rejoice.
>
> You will be sorrowful,
> But your sorrow will turn to joy.
>
> When a woman is in travail, she has sorrow,
> Because her hour has come.
>
> But when she delivers the infant, she no longer remembers
>   anguish,
> Through the joy that a human is born into the world.
>
> So you have sorrow now,
> But I will see you again,
> And your hearts will rejoice,
> And no one will take your joy from you.
>
> In that day you will ask nothing of Me.
> Truly, truly, I say to you,
> If you ask anything of the Father,
> He will give it to you in My name.
>
> Until now you have asked nothing in My name;
> Ask, and you will receive, that your joy may be full.
> (John 16:20–24)

The last time the Fourth Evangelist uses "joy," he portrays Jesus praying to the Father: "But now I am coming to You.

And these (words) I speak in the world, that they may have
My joy fulfilled in themselves" (17:13).

The Poet Laureate of Earliest Christianity, the one who
composed the poetic gems in the *Earliest Christian Hymnbook*,
also perceived that the Lord was his "joy" (*Ode* 15:1). He was
convinced that his way was "beautiful" because his "joy is the
Lord," and his "course is towards Him" (*Ode* 7:2).

This author, whether he was a Jew or a Jew who
believed in Jesus as the Messiah, expressed this conviction
because "there is a Helper for me, the Lord" (*Ode* 7:3). Who
is this "Helper"? Possibly, with the authors of Psalms 10, 30,
and 54, the Odist imagined God as the "Helper." Or perhaps,
with Christians and the author of Hebrews 13:6 who recited
Psalm 117:6 from the Greek translation, he confessed that
the Lord, or God, was "my Helper." As will become clear,
the Poet was most likely a Jew who came to believe in Jesus'
Messiahship.

I am grateful to Heather Carraher for the layout of
this book and to Cascade Books for publishing my work. I
am indebted to Jim Joyner and Brian Rhea who helped me
proof what I had written. I salute Dr. Chuck Fromm for his
focus on the *Odes of Solomon* and the launching of The Odes
Project (see www.theodesproject.com). Some of the costs
of preparing this work were covered by a grant from the
Foundation on Judaism and Christian Origins. I am grateful
for this support.

Over 35 years ago, I published the Syriac edition of
the *Odes of Solomon* (Oxford: Clarendon Press, 1973). This
year, 2009, marks the one-hundredth anniversary of the
discovery by J. Rendel Harris of the *Odes* and *Psalms of
Solomon* in a Syriac manuscript that he found in his office.
In the "Introduction" you can read and share his excitement.
I am pleased these *Odes* are being put to music and sung, or
chanted, in cathedrals and churches around the globe. May
we all move ahead into the unseen future by putting on "the
love of the Lord," as the Odist imagined.

JHC
30 May 2009
Princeton

Introductory Reflections

Two millennia ago a gifted poet in the Middle East composed the Earliest Christian Hymnbook. It is called the *Odes of Solomon*. The ancient Semite is the anonymous Odist, the poet laureate of Earliest Christianity.

Having studied the *Odes* since 1966, I believe the Odist received unique spiritual truths. His poetry explodes out of the genius of Jesus' Judaism and the energy released upon those who experienced God's resurrection of Jesus. Having ascended Mount Sinai and seeing the sun rise behind mountains thousands of miles to the East, and hearing the elevated worship of many in Greek, German, English, Hebrew, and Arabic, I sense that the Odist lived on the highest mountain peaks and shares with us his own moments of experiencing God before a burning bush.

The Odist is familiar to me. I seem to know him and share some of his experiences (as you probably have). With him I have seen fruits that are "full, even complete" in spring; I remember stopping, during a walk near the Jordan River, to examine pomegranates and other ripe fruits hanging invitingly from trees. It is easy to imagine with him that these "are full of Your salvation" (1:5). I have held in my hands the remains of burned timbers from the Temple Mount that went up into conflagration in 70 CE, and with the Odist I can affirm:

> No man can desecrate Your holy site, O my God;
> Nor can he alter it, and put it in another site.
> Because (he has) no power over it;
> For Your sanctuary You designed before You made special
> sites. (*Ode* 4:1–2)

Similar to the poetic vision in the Revelation of John, the Odist's words represent a subtle condemnation of the

Roman Emperor, Titus, who allowed the Temple and most of its treasures to disappear into smoke.

I can envision the Odist listening to the playing of a harp and imagining fresh poetry:

> As the [wind] moves through a harp
> And the strings speak,
> So the Spirit of the Lord speaks through my members,
> And I speak through His love. (*Ode* 6:1–2).

Experiencing a desert storm (a *hamzin*) in the Judean desert, facing death in the blazing heat in the loathsome shallows of the Dead Sea, coming up out of the Negev, exhausted and thirsty, fearing thirst would not be quenched, and yearning for the cool water and shade of Ein Gedi, I can appreciate the means by which the Odist expressed our eschatological hope:

> Then all the thirsty upon the earth drank,
> And thirst was relieved and quenched. (*Ode* 6:11)

Such thoughts do help us imagine a spring gushing forth its water (*Ode* 40:2) so we might "rest beside the spring;" the Lord's spring is indeed "pleasing and sparkling." This water is most "refreshing" (*Ode* 30:2–4).

Bending over to pick up a piece of marble from the first century in the Mediterranean near Caesarea Maritima and walking beside the Sea of Galilee in the predawn or dusk, I often will spy puffs of foam generated by the strong wind. The Odist knew such foam and used it to make a point:

> And ignorance appeared like dust,
> And like the foam of the sea. (*Ode* 18:11)

In early morning on the way to excavate at Bethsaida (the home of some of Jesus' disciples), I have seen the golden sun rise over the Golan Heights, dismissing the darkness, and felt the dew of the predawn as I drove down and across the Jordan River. As I think back on these experiences I better appreciate the Odist's fondness for the sun; for him the sun symbolized the presence of God's enlightening warmth:

> And the Lord (is) like the sun
> Upon the face of the land.
>
> My eyes were enlightened,
> And my face received the dew;
>
> And my breath was refreshed
> By the pleasant fragrance of the Lord. (*Ode* 11:13–15)

These reflections appear again in *Ode* 15:

> As the sun is the joy to them who seek its daybreak,
> So my joy is the Lord;
>
> Because He is my sun,
> And His rays have restored me,
> And His light has dismissed all darkness from my face.
>   (*Ode* 15:1–2)

Having seen doves mother those in their nests in Galilee, I can appreciate the Odist feeling that "the wings of the Spirit" were over his heart "as the wings of doves over their nestlings" (*Ode* 28:1). Like Jesus from Nazareth, he was a keen observer of nature.

The Odist's analogies are similar to Jesus' parables in which metaphors and images are true to nature. Both saw the affinity between heaven and earth. Vegetation and animal life in Galilee and other areas of the Middle East can arouse emotions if one allows nature to speak about its Creator. The Spirit often moved the Poet:

> When one is surrounded entirely (by) pleasing country,
> There is nothing divided in him.
>
> The likeness of that which is below
> Is that which is above. (*Ode* 34:3–4)

With this consummate Poet, I yearn for a future that is free of the past years' troubles. With him I believe life's purpose is to find moments to praise God and yearn at all times for God's truth, as verdant fruit-bearing is the purpose of the vine and melody the purpose of the harp:

> Teach me the odes of Your truth,
> That I may produce fruits in You.
>
> And open to me the harp of Your Holy Spirit,
> So that through every note I may praise You, O Lord.
> (*Ode* 14:7–8)

With the Odist I can feel the presence of the living God and the Love that the ever-creating Creator shares with all of us. Worshipping with these *Odes* before me, I sense continuity with the Jewish geniuses who were roughly contemporaneous with Jesus, with Jesus' Judaism and its deep piety, and with Jesus and his passion for the Father. The following poetic insight seems to echo Jesus' devotion to God as Father and the Johannine concept that Jesus is the Word:

> The Father of knowledge
> Is the Word of knowledge.
>
> He who created wisdom
> Is wiser than His works. (*Ode* 7:7–8)

Helping us cultivate this unity with Jesus and with his earliest followers is the Odist's gift to each of us who wish to reconnect with our origins. We are allowed to experience our own spirituality in light of another religion, the Judaism Jesus knew. And we do so with a deep appreciation of kinship with all who love and worship the One and Only God.

The beauty of the *Odes* seems to lie in their spontaneous and joyous affirmation that the long-awaited Messiah has come to God's people:

> My joy is the Lord and my course is towards Him;
> This way of mine is beautiful.
>
> For there is a Helper for me, the Lord.
> He has generously shown Himself to me in His simplicity,
> Because His kindness has diminished His grandeur.
> (*Ode* 7:2–3)

The Complex Origin of the Hymnbook

When you read the translation of the Odist's masterpieces,
you will probably imagine that his compositions are similar
to the ode quoted by Paul in Philippians 2 and the Logos
Hymn that begins the good news according to the Fourth
Evangelist. You will be correct.

In all likelihood, the Odist was a Jew and may have
been an Essene as Paul had been a Pharisee. That is, the
Odist had some relationship with the Jewish sect or group
that collected and wrote "the Dead Sea Scrolls." Why? It is
because he seems to know the *Rule of the Community* (the
magna carta of the Essenes) and the *Thanksgiving Hymns*
(the hymns or odes of the Essenes). Eventually, he believed
that Jesus was the long-awaited Messiah (see *Ode* 24).

The Odist's poetry is similar to the Psalter, the Psalms
of David. He often bases his odes or psalms on the Psalter,
but unlike the Davidic Psalter he includes no lament
in his collection that he may have attributed to David's
son, Solomon. The spirituality of the *Odes* breathes an
enthusiastic joy at the dawning of a new day. Why? It is
because the Odist believes the Messiah has finally appeared.

Although the collection is "Christian," some *Odes*
appear to be Jewish; that is, nothing uniquely Christian is
found in some *Odes*; the thought in them is profoundly
Jewish, and celebration is directed to God or the Most
High. The Odist composed his poetic masterpieces when
many of those who believed in Jesus were Jews and
when there had been no parting of the ways between
"Christians" and "Jews." While almost everything Jewish
can be Christian (as in the poetry of the Lord's Prayer), not
everything Christian can be Jewish (as the exaltation of the
Messiah on the cross).

While the collection is Christian, some *Odes* appear
Jewish, perhaps composed before the Odist believed in
Jesus' Messiahship. Others may mirror a proto-Gnosticism,
an ancient belief that salvation is achieved through personal
knowledge; such ideas are also found in the Gospel of John

and other inspired compositions that were not included in the canon, such as the *Gospel of Thomas*, the *Hymn of the Pearl*, and the *Gospel of Truth*. Using these definitions and perceptions, here is a list of the character of each *Ode* (forty are extant in Syriac [a Semitic language similar to Aramaic, Jesus' language], five in Coptic [*Pistis Sophia*], one in Greek, and one quotation in Latin):

NO.	THEME	CHARACTER
1	My Wreathed-Crown	Jewish [in *Pistis Sophia*]
2	[lost]	
3	The Beloved	Christian? [not Gnostic]
4	God's Sanctuary	Christian [heavily Jewish]
5	Praising the Lord for Grace and Salvation	Jewish! [in *Pistis Sophia*]
6	Praising His Holy Spirit	Jewish [not Gnostic]
7	The Course of Joy	Christian! [not Gnostic]
8	Fruits of the Lord	Christian [not Gnostic]
9	The Wreathed- Crown of the True Covenant	Jewish [not Gnostic]
10	The Fruit of the Lord's Peace	Christian
11	The Lord's Paradise	Proto-Gnostic [?] very Jewish [in Greek]
12	The Ineffable Word	Christian [not Gnostic]
13	The Lord Is Our Mirror	Jewish or Christian
14	The Odes of Your Truth	Jewish
15	The Lord Is My Sun	Jewish
16	My Work Is The Lord's Psalm	Jewish
17	My Wreathed-Crown Is Living	Christian [heavily Jewish]
18	The Love of the Most High	Jewish
19	The Cup of Milk	Christian! [Latin quotation]
20	A Wreathed-Crown from His Tree	Jewish
21	The Lord's Grace	Jewish [not Gnostic]

NO.	THEME	CHARACTER
22	The Holy Ones' Dwelling Place	Christian! [in *Pistis Sophia*]
23	Joy Is for the Elect Ones	Christian!
24	Our Lord Messiah	Christian!
25	My Helper	Jewish, Christian [in *Pistis Sophia*]
26	The Odists Stand in Serenity	Jewish and Christian
27	The Upright Cross	Christian!
28	Immortal Life Embraced Me	Christian
29	The Lord Is My Hope	Christian
30	The Lord's Living Spring	Jewish, Christian, and Proto-Gnostic
31	Immortal Life	Christian!
32	Joy from the Heart	Christian
33	The Perfect Virgin Is Judge	Christian!
34	The Simple Heart	Proto-Gnostic and Christian
35	The Lord's Dew	Christian
36	The Lord's High Place	Christian
37	The Lips of My Heart	Christian
38	The Light of Truth	Proto-Gnostic and Christian
39	The Lord's Power	Christian [not Gnostic]
40	The Lord's Odes of Immortality	Christian [very Jewish]
41	Our Hearts Mediate in His Love	Christian!
42	The Righteous One: Our Savior	Christian!

The "Christian" *Odes* are extremely close to the types of Jewish thought that were known in the Holy Land before 136 CE. This dimension contrasts with the anti-Judaism that abounds in the New Testament Apocrypha and Pseudepigrapha (gospels and related works not included in the canon) and some other early Christian compositions. It also distinguishes the *Odes* from the two most Jewish

Introduction

Gospels, Matthew and John, since these Gospels reflect
conflicts with other Jewish groups, especially the tensions
among Jews after the First Jewish War of 66–73/4. It is
odd that the *Odes* discerned to be Proto-Gnostic are
not excerpted by the author of the *Pistis Sophia*. Long
after the Odist, this author used excerpts from the *Odes*,
impressively those that seem Jewish, as prophecies by
Solomon (*Pistis Sophia* 114).

What is the significance of the observation that the
list shifts to being almost completely Christian beginning
with *Ode* 27 and that *Odes* 13 through 21 (except 19) are
basically Jewish?

With these preliminary comments on the complex and
diverse symbolic theology in the Hymnbook, we can now
introduce the most likely conclusions regarding the origin
of these fascinating and mystical poems or odes.

Texts

One hundred years ago, the famous Syriac scholar J.
Rendel Harris made an unusual discovery. You may
share the excitement, listening to his own words which
were published in "An Early Christian Hymn-Book,"
Contemporary Review 95 (1909) 414–28:

> On the 4th of January last, having a little leisure time,
> I thought I would devote it to sorting and identifying
> a heap of torn and stained paper leaves written in the
> Syriac language, which had been lying on my shelves
> for a long time, waiting for attention and not finding it.
> Amongst them was a bunch of leaves which I took to
> be a late copy of the conventional Syriac Psalter. It was
> divided by rubrics, which numbered a series of psalms,
> such as *Psalm four, Psalm five* and so on, down to *Psalm
> sixty.* The conventional Psalter was suggested by the
> fact that a number of them were marked for choral use
> by the addition of the first letter of the word Hallelujah
> to the successive stanzas. This is a not uncommon
> feature in Syriac Psalters. Without any suspicion of
> anything out of the common, I began to examine the

text in a leisurely manner, and was presently surprised
to find that it was not our regular Hebrew Psalter, but
something quire different.

Eventually, Harris was surprised to discover the *Psalms of
Solomon* and something further: "Examination also showed
that at the beginning of the new book could be found every
one of the passages which had been quoted" in the *Pistis
Sophia*. He continues: "Further examination showed the
very psalm or ode quoted by Lactantius. And since the
whole book, with the exception of slight mutilations at the
beginning and ending, represented a collection of sixty
or sixty-one psalms, it was evident that between two and
three times as much Solomonic matter was now to hand as
we possessed formerly." What had Harris discovered one
hundred years ago? Here are his words: "We have shown
that we have undoubtedly recovered the lost book of the
Psalms and Odes of Solomon." It is appropriate at this time
to publish a popular edition of the *Odes*, since this is the
centennial of the discovery of the *Odes*.

Today, we know that the Earliest Christian
Hymnbook, the *Odes of Solomon*, is preserved in four
manuscripts: two are in Syriac but neither preserves the
whole collection of the *Odes*. One manuscript is in Greek,
but it preserves only one ode, *Ode* 11. And one is in Coptic;
it consists of excerpts from five *Odes* in the *Pistis Sophia* (a
fourth-century work of Egyptian Christianity). The *Odes*
are quoted only in the early fourth century by Lactantius,
who quoted in Latin part of *Ode* 19 (*Div. Inst.* 4.12.3).

Not all of the original 42 *Odes* are extant. *Ode* 1 is
most likely preserved in a Coptic citation in the *Pistis
Sophia*; but all of *Ode* 2 and the beginning of *Ode* 3 are
lost. The collection was perhaps attributed by the Odist to
Solomon. It is characterized by the joy and love experienced
at the appearance of the Beloved who is the Messiah (*Ode*
7:1–2). Because of God's revelation through the Prophet
Nathan, Solomon was hailed as "Jedidiah," that is "Beloved
of the Lord" (cf. 2 Samuel 12:25).

Original Language

The original language of the *Odes of Solomon* is perhaps Greek, but most likely an early form of Aramaic-Syriac. The extant Greek preserves Semitisms that suggest an earlier manuscript in Syriac, or better Aramaic-Syriac. The Syriac texts abound in the careful use of words (notably paronomasia and assonance), rhythm, and other linguistic features that indicate the scribe was either an unusually gifted translator or more likely composing these *Odes* in an early form of Aramaic-Syriac.

Date

Specialists on the *Odes* now agree that the collection was completed in the early second century, and most likely before 125 CE. The Greek manuscript (Bodmer Papyrus XI), which dates from the third century CE, was copied from an earlier Greek manuscript that most likely takes us back into the second century CE. That is evident since the scribe inadvertently omits, and later adds in the margins, a portion of the ode. If the original language is not Greek, then we must allow for some time for the *Odes* to be composed and then later translated into Greek. If the *Odes* as a collection predates 125, then the question now to be researched is the date of each ode in the collection. What is the date of the earliest ode in the collection? It is clear that the hymns in a hymnbook were composed over a considerable period and years before they were assembled into a hymnbook.

Place of Origin

Long before the *Odes* were composed, the first world culture appeared; it was the Hellenistic World. Commerce and the movement of ideas traveled from Parthia in the East to Rome in the West and even on to Spain. After the end of the first century BCE, piracy on the high seas was abolished and substantial roads still evident in places today

connected the East with the West. Since there were no
barriers to the trafficking of concepts and expressions in
the Middle East, it is not easy to discern the place in which
a document was composed. The situation applies especially
to most documents composed between the death of Herod
in 4 BCE and the death of Bar Kokhba in 136 CE.

If the *Odes* were composed in Greek, they could
have been written virtually anywhere in the Middle East,
including Egypt, Syria, and Palestine. If they were composed
in Aramaic-Syriac, then they may have been composed in
the Holy Land, perhaps in Galilee, or elsewhere in western
Syria. As when assessing most scriptural works on the
fringes of a canon that is still open in the second century
CE, scholars find it practically impossible to discern the
place in which a document was composed.

Perhaps one may offer reflections that are speculative.
The obvious affinities between these *Odes* and the Gospel
of John make the Holy Land, Ephesus, Antioch, and even
western Syria (in the early second century), a likely place
of origin. The parallels with the sectarian Dead Sea Scrolls,
and the Gospel of John, and links with Ignatius of Antioch
support the hypothesis that the *Odes* may have been
composed in or near Antioch or somewhere in western
Syria.

Relation to the Old Testament

As a poet only echoes sources, so the Odist only alludes
to the books in the Old Testament (or Hebrew Bible). *Ode*
6 reflects Ezekiel 47, and *Ode* 22:9 echoes Ezekiel 37:4–6.
Ode 41:9 may be dependent on Proverbs 8:22. *Ode* 8:19
seems influenced by Isaiah 58:8, and *Ode* 16:12 by Genesis
2:2. The Odist is deeply and undeniably influenced by the
Psalter; he seems to know it in Hebrew and Greek. *Odes*
7:10 and 9:8–9 are apparently influenced by the Greek of
Psalms 50:3 [Hebrew 51:1] and 20:4 [Hebrew 21:3]. In at
least two places, the Odist seems to diverge from the Greek
text of the Psalter: *Odes* 5:8 and 29:10 follow the Hebrew

(or Syriac) of Psalms 21:11 and 1:4. As expected in a
Hymnbook that rejoices in the Messiah's passion, the most
influential psalm is Psalm 22; that is, *Ode* 28:14 reflects
Psalm 22:16, *Ode* 28:18 mirrors Psalm 22:18, and *Ode*
31:8–13 borrows from Psalm 22:16–18.

Most interesting is how the Odist seems to modify
passages in the Psalter that he apparently knew by heart.
Notice how he rewrites Psalm 84:10, "For a day in your
courts is better than a thousand elsewhere." He reintroduces
it as: "For one hour of Your faith / Is more excellent than all
days and years" (*Ode* 4:5). Psalm 1:2, "And on His Law they
will meditate day and night," most likely helped the Odist
with the following composition:

> And let our faces shine in His light.
> And let our hearts mediate in His love,
> By night and by day. (*Ode* 41:6)

Relation to Some Dead Sea Scrolls and Other Early Scriptures

The abundant and significant links between the *Odes*
in the Earliest Christian Hymnbook and compositions
among the Dead Sea Scrolls raise the possibility that some
Essene compositions may have influenced the Odist. The
numerous parallels are especially impressive between
the *Odes* and the Scrolls composed at Qumran, namely
the *Rule of the Community* (1QS) and the *Thanksgiving
Hymns* (1QH). The Odist's dualism (that is, the concept
that the cosmos is defined by two opposing forces) seems
to reflect the dualism developed in 1QS 3–4. In *Ode* 38,
the Odist takes the early Jewish concept of two cosmic
spirits, developed to its highest expression in the *Rule of
the Community*, and displays them as "the Truth" or "the
Beloved and His Bride" and "the Error" or "the Bride who
was corrupting" and "the Bridegroom who corrupts and is
corrupted."

The Odist's symbolism reflects that found in the
Thanksgiving Hymns. The unique opening to each hymn in

the *Thanksgiving Hymns*—"I thank you, O Lord, because"—
reappears at the beginning of *Ode* 5:

> I praise [thank] you, O Lord,
> Because I love You.

The author of the hymn in col. 16 (formerly col. 8) in
the *Thanksgiving Hymns* was influenced by Psalm 1:2 (the
righteous are "like trees planted by streams of water"); and
he envisioned the Lord planting trees, the righteous ("Trees
of Life"), for "an eternal planting." This gifted Qumranite
would have been pleased with the ending of *Ode* 38:

> And the Lord alone was praised,
> In His planting and in His cultivation.
>
> In His care and in the blessing of His lips,
> In the beautiful planting of His right hand.
>
> Hallelujah (38:20–22)

The *Odes* and the major sectarian Qumran scrolls
contain numerous shared beliefs and symbolic thoughts,
such as a consciousness of being "the Way," the dwelling
place of the Holy Ones that God has founded upon the
rock, and God's planting for His glory. The sectarian Dead
Sea Scrolls and the *Odes* in similar salvific ways reflect
the use of symbols and terms like "knowledge," "the war,"
"crown," "living water," and "the sun." Apparently, the
Odes and the Dead Sea Scrolls share more than the same
Palestinian milieu. The editor of the Greek fragment of
Ode 11, M. Testuz, concluded it was inspired in exceptional
ways by themes from the *Thanksgiving Hymns* and that
Ode 11 was the work of an Essene. Dead Sea Scrolls expert
and *Odes* scholar, J. Carmignac, concluded that the Odist
probably had been a member of the Qumran Community.
My own research suggests that the Odist may not have been
a Qumranite, but he seems to have been influenced by the
Essenes and conceivably once had been an Essene; that
is, before he believed in Jesus' Messiahship, he may have
originally been a member of one of the numerous Essene

communities that were located on the fringes of towns or cities in the Holy Land (as Philo and Josephus reported).

The Odist breathes the atmosphere of the Jewish apocalypses that were composed between 300 BCE and 100 CE. When the Odist composed *Ode* 16:13–17, he may have been influenced by *1 Enoch* 2:1—5:2 and 69:20–21 in which early Jews recorded their belief that the luminaries do not change their orbits and that the sun and moon complete their courses and do not deviate from the eternal ordinance. But I would caution against literary influence, since the theme was common in Second Temple Judaism.

Was the Odist influenced by the *Parables of Enoch* (*1 Enoch* 37–71), a Jewish apocalyptic work most likely composed in Galilee just before Jesus' public ministry? The Odist imagines the naming of the Messiah as the Son of Man and his elevation. Note the words the Odist attributes to the Messiah:

> (The Spirit) brought Me forth before the Lord's face.
> And because I was the Son of Man,
> I was named the Light, the Son of God. (*Ode* 36:3)

During this elevation through naming, the Son of Man who is now the Son of God receives his anointing, his Messiahship: "And He anointed Me with His perfection; /And I became one of those who are near Him" (*Ode* 36:6). The Odist's imagination seems influenced by the scene found only in the *Parables of Enoch* in which Enoch sees "the throne of glory" and "the fountain of righteousness" and then:

> At that hour, that Son of Man was given a name, in the
> presence of the Lord of the Spirits, the Before-Time;
> even before the creation of the sun and the moon,
> before the creation of the stars, he was given a name in
> the presence of the Lord of the Spirits."
> (*1 Enoch* 48:2–3; E. Isaac in *OTP* 1.35).

It seems likely that the Odist knew the traditions preserved in the *Parables of Enoch*.

With the authors of *1 Enoch*, *4 Ezra*, and *2 Baruch*, and also with Jesus from Nazareth, the Odist perceives present crises in terms of the promising world above and the world to come. With the early Jewish apocalypticists, he imagines ascending into heaven and seeing the world below: "I went up into the light of Truth as into a chariot, / And Truth led me and allowed me to proceed" (*Ode* 38:1).

Relation to the Documents in the New Testament

The *Odes* were composed before documents were collected into a corpus, the New Testament, and we should not expect the Odist, as a poet, to quote from these documents. Yet, scholars have rightly perceived traditions preserved in the New Testament are evident in this Hymnbook. The traditions that Jesus was born of a Virgin appear in *Ode* 19, his baptism in *Ode* 24, and his walking on the water in *Ode* 39. Jesus' Passion and Crucifixion seem mirrored in *Odes* 8:5; 27:1–3; 28:9–20; 31:8–13; and 42:1–2. The tradition preserved in Matthew 16:18 ("And on this rock I will build my church") seems reflected in *Ode* 22:

> And the foundation of everything is Your rock.
> And upon it You built Your kingdom.
> And it became the dwelling place of the holy ones. (22:12).

The most striking and significant parallels between the *Odes* and a New Testament document are with the Gospel of John. Both contain the Word Christology (that is, both portray Jesus as the pre-existent Word who took on flesh in human space and time). Both place an emphasis on love, and the reception of eternal life through the drinking of "living water." One of the premier experts on the *Odes* today, M. Lattke, is correct in pointing out the extreme importance of the *Odes* for studying the origins of the documents in the NT.

Introduction

Jewish, Christian, Gnostic?

Some excellent scholars claimed that the *Odes* were originally Jewish but later edited by a Christian (especially Harnack) or Jewish-Christian as now extant (Harris and Mingana). Some specialists were convinced the *Odes* should be declared to be Gnostic (Gunkel and Rudolph). Most scholars contend that they are Christian (Charlesworth and Emerton). Strictly speaking, the labels "Jewish," "Gnostic," and "Christian" are ill-suited to this early Christian hymnbook attributed to Solomon. As already indicated, some passages are deeply Jewish, others apparently proto-Gnostic, and yet others influenced by Christian ideas and teachings. Thus, the *Odes* seem to have been composed when Judaism, Gnostic ideas (not Gnosticism after 150 CE), and belief in Jesus' Messianic stature are mixing easily. Clearly, it is evident that the Odist is a Jew who eventually believed that Jesus is the Messiah. As some of the leading experts on the *Odes*, namely H. Chadwick and J. Emerton, have concluded and I have emphasized, the *Odes* should not be branded as "Gnostic" and thus dated later than 125 CE. J. H. Bernard introduced the claim that the *Odes* were composed by a Christian for baptismal services, and R. Murray has shown that this hypothesis is attractive but needs modification. Some *Odes* seem perfect for baptismal services (that is, *Odes* 1; 4:10; 6:11–18; 9:11–12; 11; 15; 17:1–5 etc.) and others reflect other settings, including the celebration of the Eucharist (*Ode* 19).

The Messiah in the Odes

Let us now note how "the Messiah" is mentioned in the *Odes*. The references to the Messiah are not influenced by developed Christian concepts; they rather are closer to the brilliant messianic reflections by Jews before 70 CE. In *Ode* 9:3 the Odist mentions "the Messiah" for the first time:

> The word of the Lord and His desires,
> The holy thought which He has thought concerning His Messiah.

This thought is fundamentally Jewish. The mention of "His Messiah" (which appears also in *Ode* 41:3–4) is reminiscent of "His Messiah" of the *Psalms of Solomon*. This late first-century BCE hymnbook composed in Jerusalem subordinates the Messiah to the Lord, Yahweh (cf. *Psalms of Solomon* 18:5).

Who is "the Lord" in the *Ode*? Is "the Lord" the Creator, Yahweh, Jesus from Nazareth, or a conflation of various terms or titles, and how do we know that? On the one hand, no one should imagine that the Odist denied Jesus' divinity. The Odist is very close to the Christology in the Gospel of John, always stressing the oneness between the Messiah and the Father. On the other hand, in antiquity non-believing Jews (those who did not believe in Jesus) would have taken the noun to refer to Yahweh. Thus, it is not wise to label the Odist as a "Christian" without reflection, discussion, and clarification.

In *Ode* 17:17, the noun "Messiah" appears in a doxology:

> Glory to you, our Head,
> O Lord Messiah.
>
> Hallelujah

A Jew, expecting the coming of the Messiah, or a Christian could have recited this doxology. Perhaps we should rethink early worship services. Since some early Roman objects have a Christian cross and a Jewish menorah, and since synagogues and churches were often in the same area of a town or city, it is likely that some Jews and Christians worshipped together. In the late fourth century, John Chrysostom, the bishop of Constantinople, even berated Christians for attending synagogue services. Again, we should recall that the Jew who composed the *Psalms of Solomon* called the Messiah "the Lord Messiah" (*Psalms of Solomon* 17:32; 18:7). If the *Odes* are to be labeled "Christian," then we need to also stress that the Christianity of the *Odes* is reflected so that some Jews could join in chanting them. As Jews and Christians today reflect on such scenarios, it is good to affirm our common heritage, as siblings of the same mother.

In contrast to the apocryphal New Testament compositions, which are frequently anti-Jewish, the *Odes* are not anti-Jewish; in fact they are sometimes anti-Gentile (cf. *Ode* 10:4–6).

In *Ode* 24:1 the Odist reveals his Messianic belief:

> The dove fluttered over the head of our Lord Messiah,
> Because He was her Head.

Again, "Lord Messiah" is mentioned, but there is no clear reference to Jesus (whose name never appears in the *Odes*). This passage, however, appears to be a poetic reflection on the baptism of Jesus, highlighted by the descent of the spirit as a dove, which is described in the Gospels (Matthew 3:16; Mark 1:10; Luke 3:22; and John 1:32). Yet the passage is only obliquely Christian, and there seem to be innuendoes of early Gnostic belief in the exegesis of the passage in the following verses. Note especially *Ode* 24:9–12:

> And all of them who were lacking perished,
> Because they were not able to express the word so that they
>   might remain.

> And the Lord destroyed the thoughts,
> Of all those who did not have the truth with them.

> For they were lacking in wisdom,
> They who exalted themselves in their mind.

> So they were rejected,
> Because the truth was not with them.

We do not know much about the breadth of Christian beliefs at the turn of the first to the second centuries CE. Some scholars may argue that we should expect a Christian to stress that the Messiah is the one who brings salvation and peace to those on earth. Instead, the Odist stresses the Messiah brings punishment to those who are lacking

in wisdom. This idea seems strange in light of the early
Christian confession that the Messiah brings the truth or
is the truth (cf. John 14:6). Thus, these verses in *Ode* 24 do
seem quasi-Gnostic or maybe naively Gnostic; however,
if this Ode seems not to sufficiently stress some Christian
claims, it is also far from Gnosticism.

In *Ode* 39:11–12 we find another allusion—again
veiled—to another aspect of the charismatic dimension or
pneumatic quality of Jesus' life, according to the Gospels:

> On this side and on that the waves were lifted up,
> But the footsteps of our Lord Messiah stood firm.
>
> And they are not blotted out;
> Neither are they destroyed. (*Ode* 39:11–12)

Obviously, readers today who are familiar with the New
Testament will see an allusion to the account of Jesus'
walking on the water, which is found in Matthew 14:22–33;
Mark 6:45–52; and John 6:16–21 (but not in Luke). Again,
the allusion is only oblique and the mention of the Messiah
is to our "Lord Messiah" (cf. "the Lord Messiah" in the
Psalms of Solomon 17:32 and 18:7).

The Odist mentions the Messiah twice in his next to
last poem, *Ode* 41:

> We live in the Lord by his grace,
> And life we receive by his Messiah.
>
> For a great day has shined upon us,
> And wonderful is he who has given to us of his glory. (*Ode*
>   41:3–4)
>
> The Man who humbled himself,
> But was raised because of his own righteousness.
>
> The Son of the Most High appeared
> In the perfection of his Father.
>
> And light dawned from the Word
> That was before time in him.
>
> The Messiah in truth is one.

> And he was known before the foundations of the world,
> That he might give life to persons forever by the truth of His
>   name. (*Ode* 41:12–15)

As in *Ode* 9:3, so here we hear about "His Messiah"
(cf. *Psalms of Solomon* 18:5). *Ode* 41 is clearly the most
"Christian" interpretation of the Messiah in the *Odes*.
Especially note the joyous crescendo at the appearance
of the Messiah, the poetic vision of Jesus' humility or
crucifixion, the Sonship Christology, and the Word
Christology (similar to the preexistence of the Word
in the Prologue of the Gospel of John). Yet, the name
"Jesus" does not appear here or anywhere in the *Odes*.
The thin veneer of Christian theology seems pro-Jewish
and contrasts markedly with the growing hostility to
"Jews" in Matthew and John (that is, gospels written just
before or contemporaneous with the composition of
some *Odes*). If one needs a label for the Odist, I would
suggest: a Jew, perhaps once an Essene, who was ecstatic
about the appearance of God's Messiah, whose sacrifice
and righteousness brought love and life to all who have
knowledge (see *Odes* 8:8–12; 9:7; 11:4; 12:3 etc.) and love
the Lord (see *Odes* 3:3–5; 5:1; 6:2; 8:20–22; etc).

Importance

The importance of the *Odes* is obvious. They indicate a fork
in the road in the development of Western culture. The
Odist seems to stand at a three-way junction: Some on the
way will proceed ahead to Rabbinic Judaism, others will
move on to full-blown Gnosticism, and many will progress
to orthodox Christianity.

Of singular importance is the symbolism in the
Earliest Christian Hymnbook that will help restore the
feminine in conception and worship—a dimension of
theology judged lacking by many scholars. Those who
have given us our sacred Scriptures emphasized that God
created both male and female, disclosing that the human
was in God's image. Jesus revealed that in the life after

death there is no more distinction between male and female; all will be like the angels in heaven. Paul informs us that in Christ we are neither male nor female. These important theological insights help us appreciate that each human reflects the Creator who represents all categories, including the masculine and the feminine. The earliest Christians represented the feminine aspect of the divinity by the Virgin Mary. Among Christians who worshipped in Aramaic and Syriac, the Holy Spirit was perceived to be feminine.

The Odist perceived the Spirit to be feminine, and also describes the Father with feminine imagery (most likely to warn against imaging God as a male or a warrior god). Moreover, in *Ode* 19 the Odist refers to the Father whose "breasts were full" (19:3). As E. Kingsmill has shown recently, the Odist most likely borrowed this imagery from the Song of Songs 1:2 and 1:4, a composition also ascribed to Solomon. Kingmill's insight is accurate, according to the version of the pre-70 Hebrew manuscripts that have no vowels or vowel signs, as well as by the Septuagint (the Greek translation of the Old Testament) and other ancient versions: "The Song of Songs, which is from Solomon. Let him kiss me with the kisses of his mouth; for my breasts are better than wine" (Song 1:1–2; Greek version). By the time of the Odist, many Jews and Christians assumed that the Song of Songs, "the superlative song," was the wise composition by Solomon and that Israel is the bride, and God, the Lover, the one who has "breasts." An initial shock at an unfamiliar image will hopefully be replaced by perception and appreciation of insights that transcend the physical when reading such words as these:

> The Holy Spirit opened Her bosom,
> And mixed the milk of the two breasts of the Father.
> (*Ode* 19:4).

While the author of the *Parables of Enoch* believed the Son of Man would be the Judge, the Odist transferred the function to a woman:

Introduction

However the perfect Virgin stood,
Who was preaching and summoning and saying:

"O you sons of men, return,
And you their daughters, come. . .

And I will enter into you,
And bring you forth from destruction,
And make you wise in the ways of truth. . . .

Hearken unto Me and be saved,
For I am proclaiming unto you the grace of God

And through Me you will be saved and become blessed,
I am your judge." (*Ode* 33:5–11)

The Earliest Christian Hymnbook thus provides foundational images that will help us appreciate both the masculine and the feminine elements in spirituality. The Odist may serve us well in helping us recover the feminine in our lives and worship.

One final word focused on the beauty of the *Odes* summarizes the mystical grandeur of these early poems. Their attractiveness seems to lie in the spontaneous and joyous affirmations that the long-awaited Messiah has come to God's people:

My joy is the Lord and my course is towards Him;
This way of mine is beautiful.

For there is a Helper for me, the Lord.
He has generously shown Himself to me in His simplicity,
Because His kindness has diminished His grandeur.

He became like me, that I might receive Him.
In form He was considered like me, that I might put Him on.

And I trembled not when I saw Him.
Because He was gracious to me.

Like my nature He became, that I might understand Him.
And like my form, that I might not turn away from Him.
    (*Ode* 7:2–6)

Many, especially Christians, today will feel in the Odist's verses a reference to the incarnation. They may also experience acceptance in the power of the Messiah:

> The Son of the Most High appeared
> In the perfection of His Father.
>
> And light dawned from the Word
> That was before time in Him.
>
> The Messiah in truth is one.
> And He was known before the foundations of the world,
> That He might give life to persons forever by the truth of His
> name. (*Ode* 41:13–16)

Conclusion

I hope you, as one dedicated to God, will take more seriously the Jewish origins of a movement that became Christianity; but most importantly, I wish you will grow closer to our Creator by meditating on these spiritual gems. As one who believes in God as the Source of love, you are invited to join the Odist in chanting:

> I am putting on [the love of the Lord] . . .
>
> For I should not have known how to love the Lord,
> If He had not loved me continuously.
>
> Who is able to distinguish love?
> (Surely, it is) only the one who is loved.
>
> I love the Beloved and I myself love Him;
> And where His rest is, there am I also. (*Ode* 3:1–5)

Perhaps these preliminary reflections will help you perceive that the Odist is the Poet Laureate of Earliest Christianity. As you meditate on the Poet's creations, I hope you will be refreshed "from the living water that does not die" (*Ode* 11:7) that overflows to all who love the Lord. When despondent and depressed, and unable to appreciate that we are "saved by Your grace" (*Ode* 25:4), each of us might find solace in the promise:

Introduction

You who were despised, from henceforth be raised,
For your Righteousness has been raised;

For the right hand of the Lord is with you,
And He will be Your Helper. (*Ode* 8:5–6)

On final reflection, the Odist would wish us to be contemplative and realize that the closer we draw to God the more we feel incapable of expressing our wonder and devotion:

Who can interpret the wonders of the Lord?
Though he who interprets should perish,
Yet that which was interpreted will remain.

For it suffices to perceive and be satisfied,
For the Odists stand in serenity;

Like a river which has an increasingly gushing spring,
And flows to the relief of them that seek it. (*Ode* 26:11–13)

Selected Bibliography

Bernard, J. H. *The Odes of Solomon*. Texts and Studies 8.3. Cambridge: Cambridge University Press, 1912.

Carmignac, J. "Un qumrânien converti au christianisme: L'Auteur des Odes de Salomon." In *Qumran-Probleme*, edited by H. Bardtke, 75–108. Deutsche Akademie der Wissenschaften zu Berlin 42. Berlin: Akademie-Verlag, 1963.

Chadwick, H. "Some Reflections on the Character and Theology of the Odes of Solomon." In *Kyriakon: Festschrift Johannes Quasten*, edited by P. Granfield and J.A. Jungmann, 1:266–70. Münster: Aschendorff, 1970.

Charlesworth, J. H. *Critical Reflections on the Odes of Solomon: Volume 1: Literary Setting, Textual Studies, Gnosticism, the Dead Sea Scrolls and the Gospel of John*. Journal for the Study of the Pseudepigrapha, Supplement Series 22 (The Distinguished Scholars Collection). Sheffield: Sheffield Academic, 1998.

———. "The Naming of the Son of Man, the Light, the Son of God: How the *Parables of Enoch* May Have Influenced the *Odes of Solomon*." In *"I Sowed Fruits into Hearts" (Odes Sol. 17:13): Festschrift for Professor Michael Lattke*, edited by P. Allen, M.

Introduction

Franzmann, and R. Strelan, 31–43. Early Christian Studies 12. Strathfield, NSW: St Paul's Publications, 2007.

———. *The Odes of Solomon*. Oxford: Clarendon, 1973. Reprinted, Missoula, MT: Scholars, 1977. [contains the critical text and translation as well as a bibliography to that time]

———. "The Odes of Solomon." In *The Old Testament Pseudepigrapha*, edited by J. H. Charlesworth, 2:725–71. Garden City, NY: Doubleday, 1985.

———, editor. *Papyri and Leather Manuscripts of the Odes of Solomon*. Dickerson Series of Photographs 1. Durham, NC: Hunter, 1981.

———. "Qumran, John and the Odes of Solomon." In *John and Qumran*, edited by J. H. Charlesworth, 107–36. London: Chapman, 1972.

Emerton, J. A. "The Odes of Solomon." In *The Apocryphal Old Testament*, edited by H. F. D. Sparks, 683–731. Oxford: Clarendon, 1984.

———. "Some Problems of Text and Language in the Odes of Solomon." *Journal of Theological Studies* 18 (1967) 372–406.

Gunkel, H. "Salomo Oden." In *Die Religion in Geschichte und Gegenwart*, 5:87–90. 2nd ed. Tübingen: Mohr Siebeck, 1931.

Harnack, A., and J. Fleming. *Ein jüdisch-christliches Psalmbuch aus dem ersten Jahrhundert*. Texte und Untersuchungen 34.4. Leipzig: Hinrichs, 1910.

Harris, J. R., and A. Mingana. *The Odes of Solomon*. 2 vols. London: Longmans Green & Co., 1916–1920.

Kingsmill, E. *The Song of Songs and the Eros of God: A Study in Biblical Intertextuality*. Oxford Theological Monographs. Oxford: Oxford University Press, 2009.

Lattke, M. *Die Oden Salomos in ihrer Bedeutung für Neues Testament und Gnosis*. Orbis Biblicus et Orientalis 25/1, 25/1a, 25/2, 25/3. Göttingen: Vandenhoeck & Ruprecht, 1979–1986.

———. *Oden Salomos: Text, Übersetzung, Kommentar: Teil 1 Oden 1 und 3–14*. Novum Testamentum et Orbis Antiquus 41/1. Göttingen: Vandenhoeck & Ruprecht, 1999.

Murray, R. "Recent Studies in Early Symbolic Theology." *Heythrop Journal* 6 (1965) 412–33.

———. *Symbols of Church and Kingdom: A Study in Early Syriac Tradition*. London: T. & T. Clark, 2006.

Rudolph, K. "War der Verfasser der Oden Salomos ein 'Qumran-Christ'? Ein Beitrag zur Diskussion um die Anfänge der Gnosis." *Revue de Qumran* 4 (1964) 523–55.

Testuz, M. *Papyrus Bodmer X–XII: XI: Onzième Ode de Salomon*. Cologny-Genève: Bibliotheca Bodmeriana, 1959.

The wreathed-crown

of truth is plaited

for me

MY WREATHED-CROWN

1   Like a wreathed-crown on my head is the Lord,
And never shall I be without Him.

2   The wreathed-crown of truth is plaited for me,
Causing Your branches to blossom within me,

3   For it is not like a parched crown
That fails to blossom.

4   But You have lived upon my head,
And You have blossomed upon me.

5   Your fruits are full, even complete;
They are full of Your salvation.

ODE 2

Lost

THE BELOVED

1   . . .
     I am putting on [the love of the Lord].[a]

2   And His members are with Him,
     And I am dependent on them; and He loves me.

3   For I should not have known how to love the Lord,
     If He had not loved me continuously.[b]

4   Who is able to distinguish love?
     (Surely, it is) only the one who is loved.

5   I love the Beloved and I myself love Him;[c]
     And where His rest is, there am I also.[d]

6   And I shall be no (rejected) stranger,[e]
     Because no jealousy is with the Lord Most High and
          Merciful.

7   I have been united (to Him), because the lover has
          found the Beloved;
     Because I love Him that is the Son, I shall become a
          son.

8   Indeed he who is joined to Him who is immortal,[f]
     Truly, he shall become immortal.

---

   a. Restored on analogy with *Ode* 23:3. Also see, however, *Odes* 4:6–7; 7:4; 13:3; 15:8; 20:7; 21:3; 23:1; 33:12; 39:8.
   b. Cf. 1 John 4:19.
   c. Or "and my soul (*npšy*) loves Him."
   d. Cf. John 14:2–3.
   e. Or "foreigner."
   f. Cf. John 14:19b.

The lover

has found the

Beloved

9   And he who delights in the Life^g
Will become living.^h

10   This is the Spirit of the Lord, which is not false,ⁱ
Which teaches the sons of men to know His ways.^j

11   Be wise, and understanding, and vigilant.

Hallelujah.

g. Cf. John 11:25.
h. Cf. John 11:25; also John 1:4; 5:26, 40; 10:10, 28; 14:6.
i. Cf. Titus 1:2.
j. Cf. John 14:17, 26; 15:26; 1QS 3.13—4.26.

You have given us
Your fellowship

GOD'S SANCTUARY

1 No man can desecrate Your holy site, O my God;
Nor can he alter it, and put it in another site.

2 Because (he has) no power over it;
For Your sanctuary You designed before You made
special sites.

3 The ancient one[a] shall not be desecrated by those
inferior to it.
You have given Your heart, O Lord, to Your faithful
ones.[b]

4 Never will You be idle,
Nor will You be without fruits;

5 For one hour of Your faith
Is more excellent than all days and years.[c]

6 For who shall put on Your grace[d]
And be rejected?[e]

7 Because Your sign[f] is known;
And Your creatures are known to it.

8 And Your hosts possess it;
And the elect archangels are clothed with it.

a. "The ancient one" refers to the Jerusalem Temple.
b. Or "your believers."
c. Note the inspiration and alteration of Psalm 84:10.
d. Or "goodness," "kindness."
e. Or "be despised," "be oppressed."
f. Or "seal."

9   You have given us Your fellowship,
     Not that You were in need of us,
     But always we are in need of You.

10   Sprinkle upon us Your sprinklings;
     And open Your bountiful springs
          which abundantly supply us with milk and honey.

11   For there is no regret with You;
     That You should regret anything that you have
          promised;

12   Since the end was manifest to You.

13   For that which You gave, You gave freely,
     So that no longer will You draw back and take them
          again.

14   For everything[g] was manifest to You as God,
     And was set in order from the beginning before You.

15   And You, O Lord, have made everything.[h]

     Hallelujah.

g. Or "all."
h. Or "all."

PRAISING THE LORD FOR GRACE AND SALVATION

1   I praise You, O Lord,
    Because I love You.[a]

2   O Most High, abandon me not,
    For You are my hope.

3   Freely did I receive Your grace;
    May I live by it.[b]

4   My persecutors will come,[c]
    But let them not see me.

5   Let a cloud of darkness fall[d] upon their eyes;
    And let an air of thick darkness obscure them.

6   And let them have no light to see,
    So that they cannot seize me.

7   Let their counsel[e] become dull,
    So that whatever they have conspired will return upon
        their own heads.[f]

8   For they have devised a counsel,
    But it was not for them.[g]

a. Cf. the Hodayoth formula: "I thank (or praise) You, O Lord, because . . ."

b. Or "I shall live by it." C: "through You."

c. C: "may they fall." Cf. Jeremiah 20:11.

d. C: "it covers."

e. Or "mind"; but cf. *Ode* 5:8. C: "counsel becomes powerless."

f. C: "And what they counseled, let it come upon them." Cf. Psalm 7:16.

g. C has another line: "And they were vanquished although they were powerful." This line appears to be spurious. It breaks the bicolon

9   They prepared themselves maliciously,
    But they were found to be impotent.[h]

10 Indeed my hope[i] is upon the Lord,
    And I shall not fear.

11 And because the Lord is my salvation,
    I shall not fear.[j]

12 And He is like a wreathed-crown upon my head,
    So I shall not be disturbed.

13 Even if everything should be shaken,
    I shall stand firm.

14 And though all things visible should perish,
    I shall not be extinguished;

15 Because the Lord is with me,
    And I with Him.

    Hallelujah.

---

pattern and emphasizes ideas peculiar to the Coptic recension.

h. C: "And what they have wickedly prepared has fallen upon them."

i. Or "trust," "confidence."

j. C: "You are my God, my Savior."

The Lord is my salvation

I speak through
His love

PRAISING HIS HOLY SPIRIT

1   As the [wind] moves through a harp
    And the strings speak,

2   So the Spirit of the Lord speaks through my members,
    And I speak through His love.

3   For He destroys whatever is alien.[a]
    And everything (depends) on the Lord.

4   For thus it has been from the beginning,
    And (it will be) until the end;

5   So that nothing will be contrary;
    And nothing will rise up against Him.

6   The Lord has multiplied His knowledge;
    And He was zealous that what should be known was
        given to us through His grace.

7   And His praise He gave us on account of His name;
    Our spirits praise His Holy Spirit.

8   For there went forth a stream,[b]
    And it became a river great and broad;[c]
    Indeed, it carried away everything, and it shattered,
    And brought (it)[d] to the Temple.[e]

a. Or "foreign, strange."

b. C: "a flowing off," "a stream," "an emanation."

c. Cf. Ezekiel 47:1–12; Habakkuk 2:14; Isaiah 11:9; Zechariah 14:8; and Additions to Esther F3(6) and A9(10) to *Ode* 6:8–11. The similarities are impressive, but differences are also significant.

d. A pronoun as a direct object is often assumed in Semitic documents; see *Odes* 8:7; 9:7; 19:5–6; 20:8; 23:7; 36:2; cf. *Ode* 22:10; also see Baruch 1:7, "and they sent (it) to Jerusalem" (*kai apesteilan eis Jerousalēm*). C: "It gathered all things and it turned towards the Temple."

e. Or "Indeed it carried away everything, and it shattered, and car-

9   And the restraints of men were not able to restrain it,
    Nor even the arts of them who habitually restrain
        water.

10 For it spread over the face of all the earth,
    And it filled everything.[f]

11 Then all the thirsty upon the earth drank,[g]
    And thirst was relieved and quenched;

12 For from the Most High the drink was given.

13 Blessed, therefore, are the ministers of that drink,
    Who have been entrusted with His water.[h]

14 They have refreshed the parched lips,
    And have restored[i] the paralyzed will.[j]

15 Even lives about to expire,[k]
    Were seized from Death.[l]

16 And members who had fallen,[m]
    Were restored and set up.[n]

---

ried away the Temple."

   f. C: "and it possessed all the water." Cf. Pseudo-Clement *Recognitions* 6.

   g. C: "They who were upon the dry sand drank." Cf. *1 Enoch* 48:1; John 7:37b–38.

   h. C: "The water of the Lord."

   i. Or "aroused."

   j. C: "Those who were exhausted have received joy of heart."

   k. C: "They have embraced lives (or souls, *psychai*), having poured in the breath, so that they will not die."

   l. Or "have held back from death."

   m. Or "And limbs which had collapsed . . ."

   n. C: "have caused to stand."

17   They gave power for their coming,[o]
     And light for their eyes.

18   Because everyone recognized them as the Lord's,
     And lived by the living water[p] of eternity.[q]

     Hallelujah.

o. C: "their openness."

p. Cf. John 7:37–38.

q. "Living water" is salvivic in the *Odes* (cf. 11:7; 30:1–7); and in John (cf. John 4:10–15; 7:38); Revelation (7:17; 21:6; 22:1, 17); the Qumran Scrolls (1QH^a 8.7, 16; CD 19.34); and some post-apostolic documents: Ignatius *Romans* 7:2; and *Didache* 7:1–3.

Let the Singers sing the grace of the Lord Most High

ODE 7

THE COURSE OF JOY

1   As is the course of anger over wickedness,
      So is the course of joy over the Beloved;
      And without hindrance brings in its fruits.

2   My joy is the Lord and my course is towards Him;
      This way of mine is beautiful.

3   For there is a Helper for me, the Lord.[a]
      He has generously shown Himself to me in His
          simplicity,
      Because His kindness has diminished His grandeur.[b]

4   He became like me, that I might receive Him.
      In form He was considered like me, that I might put
          Him on.

5   And I trembled not when I saw Him,
      Because He was gracious to me.

6   Like my nature He became, that I might understand
          Him,
      And like my form, that I might not turn from Him.[c]

7   The Father of knowledge[d]
      Is the Word of knowledge.[e]

---

a. The Lord or God is called "Helper" in many biblical books; cf., e.g., Psalms 10:14; Hebrews 13:6; Sirach 51:2. Contrast 2 *Enoch* 53:1.

b. Or "greatness," "dignity." Cf. Romans 5:2; Ephesians 2:18.

c. The Syriac nouns translated as "nature" and "form" also mean "natural disposition," "essence," and "image." The language here is not docetic; but see *Odes* 17:6; 28:17–18; 41:8; and 42:10.

d. Cf. 1QS 3.15.

e. Or "word of knowledge." It is difficult to be sure when "word" should be capitalized. See 4 *Ezra* 6:38; 2 *Baruch* 21:4; *Joseph and Aseneth* 12.

8   He who created wisdom[f]
     Is wiser than His works.[g]

9   And He who created me when I was not
     Knew what I would do when I came into being.

10   On account of this He was gracious to me in His
          abundant grace;
     And he allowed me to seek from Him and benefit
          from His sacrifice.

11   For He is incorruptible,
     The perfection of the worlds and their Father.

12   He has allowed Him to appear to them that are His
          own;[h]
     In order that they may recognize Him that made them,
     And not think that they came of themselves.

13   For towards knowledge He has set His way,
     He has spread it out, and lengthened it, and brought it
          to complete perfection.[i]

14   And He set over it the traces of His light.
     And it proceeded from the beginning until the end.

15   For by Him He was served;
     And He was pleased by the Son.

16   And because of His salvation, He will possess
          everything.
     And the Most High will be known by His holy ones:

17   To announce to those who have songs of the coming
          of the Lord,

f. Perhaps: "Wisdom."
g. Cf. Proverbs 8:22–23.
h. Cf. John 1:11.
i. Cf. 1QS 11.11.

That they may go forth to meet Him and may sing to
    Him,
With joy and with the harp of many tones.

18   The Seers will go before Him;
    And they will appear before Him.

19   And they will praise the Lord in His love,
    Because He is near and does see.

20   And hatred will be removed from the earth,
    And with jealousy it will be drowned.

21   Ignorance was destroyed upon it,
    Because the knowledge of the Lord came upon it.

22   Let the Singers sing the grace of the Lord Most High,
    And let them offer their songs.

23   And let their heart be like the day,
    And their gentle voices[j] like the majestic beauty[k] of the
    Lord.

24   And let there not be any person
    That is without knowledge or voice.

25   For He gave to His creation a mouth:
    To open the voice of the mouth towards Him,
    And to praise Him.

26   Praise[l] His power
    And declare His grace.

Hallelujah.

j. Or "a musical note," "gentle sound," "soft whisper."
k. Or "majestic grace."
l. Or "Confess."

Let your love
overflow from
heart to lips

FRUITS OF THE LORD

1   Open, open your hearts to the exultation of the Lord,
    And let your love overflow[a] from heart to lips.[b]

2   In order to bring forth fruits to the Lord, a holy life;[c]
    And to speak with watchfulness in His light.

3   Stand and be established,[d]
    You who once were brought low.

4   You who were in silence, speak,
    For your mouth has been opened.

5   You who were despised, from henceforth be raised,
    For your Righteousness has been raised;

6   For the right hand of the Lord is with you,
    And He will be your Helper.

7   And peace was prepared for you,
    Before what may be your war.

(Christ Speaks)[e]

8   Hear the word of truth;
    And receive the knowledge of the Most High.[f]

a. Or "abound."

b. Both imperatives are plurals in Syriac. The *Ode* may have been intended for liturgical use in early Christian services.

c. Cf. Hosea 14:2; Hebrews 13:15; 1QH[a] 1.28; *Psalms of Solomon* 15:5.

d. Or "Rise up and stand erect . . ."

e. Here and in the following *Odes* I have added this notation. It is frequently clear that the Odist speaks as the Christ. In the manuscripts no dot, word, phrase, or grammatical form clarifies the shift in speakers.

f. As in *Ode* 8:1, the imperatives are plural.

9 Your flesh may not understand what I am about to say
to you;
Nor your garment what I am about to declare to you.[g]

10 Keep My mystery,[h] you who are kept by it.
Keep My faith, you who are kept by it.

11 And understand My knowledge, you who know Me in
truth.
Love Me with affection, you who love;

12 For I turn not My face from My own,[i]
Because I know them.

13 And before they existed,
I recognized them;
And imprinted a seal[j] on their faces.

14 I fashioned their members.
And My own breasts I prepared for them,
That they might drink My holy milk and live by it.

15 I am pleased by them,
And I am not ashamed by them.

16 For My work(s) are they,
And the power of My thoughts.

17 Therefore who can stand against My work(s)?
Or who is not subject to them?

18 I willed and fashioned mind and heart.
And they are My own.
And upon My right hand I have set My elect ones.

g. Or "to show you."
h. Cf. 1QH[a] 11.10; and 1Q27.
i. Cf. John 10:14.
j. Or "sign."

19   And My righteousness goes before them.
     And they will not be deprived of My name,
     For it is with them.[k]

     (The Odist Speaks)[l]

20   Seek and increase,
     And abide in the love of the Lord;[m]

21   And you who are loved in the Beloved;
     And you who are kept in Him who lives;
     And you who are saved in Him who was saved.[n]

22   And you shall be found incorruptible in all ages,
     On account of the name of your Father.

     Hallelujah.

k. Cf. Isaiah 58:8.
l. I add this notation.
m. Cf. John 15:9–10.
n. Compare *Ode* 8:19–21 with John 15:9–10 and 17:11–12.

In the will of the
Lord is your life,
and His purpose is
eternal life

THE WREATHED-CROWN OF THE TRUE COVENANT

1   Open your ears,
    Then I shall speak to you.[a]

2   Give me yourself,
    So that I may also give you Myself;

3   The word of the Lord and His desires,
    The holy thought which He has thought concerning
        His Messiah.

4   For in the will of the Lord is your life,
    And His purpose[b] is eternal life,
    And your perfection is incorruptible.

5   Be enriched in God the Father;
    And receive the purpose of the Most High.
    Be strong and saved by His grace.

6   For I announce peace to you, His holy ones,
    So that none of those who hear[c] will fall in the war.

7   And also that those who have known Him may not
        perish,[d]
    And so that those who receive (Him) may not be
        ashamed.[e]

8   An everlasting wreathed-crown is Truth;
    Blessed are they who set it on their head.

a. The Odist addresses his audience; the pronouns and imperatives
are in the plural form.
b. Or "mind," "belief," "intelligence."
c. Or "obey."
d. Cf. John 3:16.
e. Or "confused."

9   (It is) a precious stone,
For the wars were on account of the wreathed-crown.[f]

10   But Righteousness has taken it;
And She has given it to you.

11   Put on the wreathed-crown in the true covenant of the
        Lord,
And all those who have conquered[g] will be inscribed
        in His book.[h]

12   For their book is the justification[i] which is for you,
And She sees you before Her and wills that you will be
        saved.

Hallelujah.

---

f. Cf. *Testament of Job* 40:3; Wisdom of Solomon 5:16; 1QH[a] 9.25.

g. Or "who were free from guilt," "who were declared blameless." See Revelation 3:5; 21:7.

h. Revelation 21:27.

i. Or "victory."

THE FRUIT OF THE LORD'S PEACE

1   The Lord directed my mouth by His Word,
     And opened my heart by His Light.[a]

2   And He allowed His immortal life to dwell in me,[b]
     And permitted me to proclaim the fruit of His peace:

3   To convert the lives of those who desire to come to
      Him,
     And to capture a good captivity for freedom.

     (Christ Speaks)[c]

4   I took courage, and became strong, and captured the
      world,
     And so it became mine for the glory of the Most High,
      and of God, My Father.

5   And the scattered Gentiles were gathered together;[d]
     But I was not defiled by My love (for them),
     Because they had praised Me in high places.[e]

---

a. Perhaps "word" and "light" should be capitalized.
b. Cf. John 4:14.
c. Added by me since the following words are attributed to Christ.
d. Cf. John 11:52.
e. Cf. Malachi 1:11.

6 And traces of light were set upon their heart.
And they walked according to My life and were saved;
And they became My people forever and ever.

Hallelujah.

Traces of light were set upon their heart

Blessed, O Lord,
are they who are
planted in Your land,
and who have a place
in Your Paradise

THE LORD'S PARADISE

1   My heart was pruned and its flower appeared;
Then grace sprang up in it,
And it produced fruits for the Lord.[a]

2   For the Most High circumcised me by His Holy Spirit,
Then He uncovered my inward being[b] towards Him.
And He filled me with His love.

3   And His circumcising became my salvation.
And I ran in the Way,[c] in His peace,
In the Way of truth.[d]

4   From the beginning until the end
I received His knowledge.

5   And I was established upon the rock of truth,[e]
Where He set me.

6   And speaking waters[f] touched my lips
From the spring of the Lord[g] generously.[h]

7   And so I drank and became intoxicated,
From the living[i] water that does not die.

a. G: "for God." Compare *Ode* 11:1–3 with Deuteronomy 10:16; and 30:6.

b. Literally "kidneys."

c. Cf. Acts 24:14, 22; 9:2; John 14:6; 1QS 9.19, 21; 11.11.

d. G: "I ran a way of truth in His peace." Cf. 1QS 4.17; 9.17–18; CD 3.15.

e. G: "solid rock."

f. Cf. Ignatius *Romans* 7:2.

g. Or "the fountain of the Lord"; G: "from the fountain of life of the Lord." Cf. 1QH[a] 8.14.

h. Cf. *Gospel of Thomas* 13. Cf. also Revelation 7:17.

i. G omits. Cf. John 4:10.

And my intoxication was not with ignorance;[j]
But I abandoned[k] vanity;

9 And turned toward the Most High, my God,
And was enriched by His favors.

10 And I abandoned the folly cast upon the earth,
And stripped it off and cast it from me.

11 And the Lord renewed me with His garment,
And possessed me[l] by His light.[m]

12 And from above He gave me immortal rest;[n]
And I became like the land which blossoms and
rejoices in its fruits.

13 And the Lord (is) like the sun
Upon the face of the land.

14 My eyes were enlightened,
And my face received the dew;

15 And my breath was refreshed
By the pleasant fragrance[o] of the Lord.[p]

16 And He took me to His Paradise,
Wherein is the wealth of the Lord's pleasure.[q]

j. Cf. *Ode* 38:12–15.

k. G omits.

l. G: "and He recovered me."

m. Or "Light," cf. *Ode* 36:3; 1QS 4.8. Cf. Psalm 104:2; Baruch 5:1–9.

n. Or "incorruptible rest." G: "And He enlivened me through His incorruption." Cf. Psalm 95:11; Hebrews 3:7—4:13.

o. Cf. *1 Enoch* 24:1–6.

p. G: "in the fragrance of the kindness of the Lord."

q. A similar description of Paradise appears in many documents; see *1 Enoch* 24; *2 Enoch* 8; *Apocalypse of Abraham* 21; *Sibylline Oracles* frag. 3.48–49; also note 1QH[a] 8.12–20; *Joseph and Aseneth* 2:17–20; *Liber antiquitatum biblicarum* 12:8.

16a [[I contemplated blooming and fruit-bearing trees,
And self-grown was their wreathed-crown.

16b Their branches were flourishing
And their fruits were shining;[r]
Their roots (were) from an immortal land.

16c And a river of gladness was irrigating them,
And the region around them in the land of eternal
life.]][s]

17 Then I adored the Lord,
Because of His magnificence.

18 And I said, blessed, O Lord, are they[t]
Who are planted in Your land,
And who have a place in Your Paradise;[u]

19 And who grow in the growth of Your trees,
And have passed from darkness into light.[v]

20 Behold, all[w] Your laborers are fair,
They who work good works,
And turn from wickedness to Your kindness.[x]

r. Literally "were laughing." The Greek *egelō[n]* means only "were laughing," "were deriding." The corresponding Syriac, which I believe is behind the Greek, would be *ghk*, which means not only "laughing," but also "shining."

s. Verses 16a–16c exist only in G.

t. Cf. *Psalms of Solomon* 14:2(5).

u. Cf. *Gospel of Truth* 36:35–37.

v. This imagery is widespread in early Jewish literature; cf., e.g., *Testament of Joseph* 19:3; 1QH[a] 9.26–27; *Testament of Abraham* B7; *Joseph and Aseneth* 8:10; 15:13; *3 Baruch* 6:13; *2 Enoch* 30:15; and especially 1QS 3.13–4.26. Also cf. *Didache* 1:1; *Epistle of Barnabas* 18:1—20:2.

w. G omits.

x. G: "from wickedness to kindness."

21   For they turned away from themselves the bitterness
         of the trees,[y]
      When they were planted in Your land.[z]

22   And everyone was like Your remnant.[aa]
      [[Blessed are the workers of Your water,]][ab]
      And the eternal memorial[ac] of Your faithful servants.

23   Indeed, there is much room in Your Paradise.[ad]
      And nothing in it is barren;
      Everything is filled with fruit.

24   Praise be to You, O God,
      The delight of Paradise forever.

      Hallelujah.

---

y. G: "The pungent odor of the trees is changed in Your land." Cf. *3 Baruch* 4:15.

z. G omits. Cf. 1QH[a] 8.4–26; *Liber antiquitatum biblicarum* 18:10; 23:12; 28:4.

aa. G: "And everything occurs according to Your will." Cf. Isaiah 10:19–23.

ab. The line is extant only in G.

ac. Cf. Baruch 4:5.

ad. Cf. John 14:2.

ODE 12

THE INEFFABLE WORD

1   He has filled me with words of truth,
    That I might proclaim Him.

2   And like flowing waters, truth flows from my mouth,
    And my lips declare His fruits.

3   And He has caused His knowledge to abound in me,[a]
    Because the mouth of the Lord is the true word,
    And the door of His light.[b]

4   And the Most High has given Him to His generations,[c]
    (Who are) the interpreters of His beauty,
        and the narrators of His glory,
        and the confessors of His thought,[d]
        and the preachers of His mind,
        and the teachers[e] of His works.

5   For the subtlety of the Word is inexpressible,[f]
    And like His expression[g] so also is His swiftness and
      His acuteness,
    For limitless is His path.[h]

a. Or "overflow in me."

b. "Word," "Door," and "Light" could be capitalized and the parallels to the Gospel of John would be striking; cf. John 1:1–18; 8:12; 10:7–9.

c. Or "ages," "worlds."

d. Or "purpose."

e. Literally "those who teach to be chaste."

f. Literally "there is no narration." Both "subtlety" and "swiftness" in this verse are identical in the Syriac; hence the first two lines could be translated: "For the swiftness of the Word is inexpressible,/And like His expression so also is His swiftness and his acuteness . . ."

g. Or "utterance."

h. Or "progression." Cf. Hebrews 4:12; Wisdom of Solomon 7:22–27.

6   He never falls but remains standing;
And one cannot know His descent or His way.

7   For as His work is, so is His expectation;
For He is the light and dawning of thought.

8   And by Him the generations spoke to one another,
And those that were silent acquired speech.

9   And from Him came love and harmony;[i]
And they spoke to each other whatever was theirs.

10   And they were stimulated by the Word;
And knew Him who made them,[j]
Because they were in harmony.

11   For the mouth of the Most High spoke to them.
And His exposition was swift through Him.

12   For the dwelling-place of the Word is the human;[k]
And His truth is love.

13   Blessed are they who by means of Him have
recognized[l] everything,
And have known the Lord in His truth.

Hallelujah.

---

i. Or "equality"; cf. 12:9.
j. Cf. John 1:1–18.
k. Cf. John 1:14.
l. Or "perceived."

He is the light
and dawning of
thought

Love His holiness

and put it on

THE LORD IS OUR MIRROR

1   Behold, our mirror is the Lord;[a]
      Open (your) eyes and see them in Him.

2   And learn the manner of your face,
      Then announce praises to His Spirit.

3   And wipe the paint[b] from your face;
      Then love His holiness and put it on.

4   And you will be unblemished at all times with Him.

      Hallelujah.

---

a. Cf. *Acts of John* 95.25; Wisdom of Solomon 7:26. For "mirror" cf. 2 Corinthians 3:18; and James 1:23.

b. Cf. *Acts of John* 28–29.

ODE 14

THE ODES OF YOUR TRUTH

1   As the eyes of a son upon his father,
    So are my eyes, O Lord, at all times towards You;

2   Because my breasts
    And my pleasure are with You.

3   Do not turn aside Your mercies from me, O Lord;
    And do not take Your kindness from me.

4   Stretch out to me, my Lord, at all times, Your right hand,
    And be a guide to me till the end, according to Your will.

5   Let me be pleasing before You, because of Your glory;
    And because of Your name let me be saved from the
        Evil One.[a]

6   And, O Lord, allow Your serenity to abide with me,[b]
    And the fruits of Your love.

7   Teach me the odes of Your truth,
    That I may produce fruits in You.

8   And open to me the harp of Your Holy Spirit,
    So that through every note I may praise You, O Lord.

9   And according to the multitude of Your mercies, so
        grant unto me;
    And hasten to grant our petitions.

10   For You are sufficient
    For all our needs.

    Hallelujah.

a. Or "evil." Cf. Psalm 31:3–4.
b. Or "Your gentleness."

O Lord, allow Your
serenity to abide
with me

My joy is the Lord

THE LORD IS MY SUN

1   As the sun is the joy to them who seek its daybreak,
     So my joy is the Lord;

2   Because He is my sun,
     And His rays have restored me.
     And His light has dismissed all darkness from my
        face.[a]

3   Eyes I have possessed in Him;
     And I have seen His holy day.

4   Ears I have acquired;
     And I have heard His truth.

5   The thought of knowledge I have acquired;
     And I have lived[b] fully through Him.

6   I abandoned the way of error;
     And I went towards Him and received salvation from
        Him generously.

7   And according to His generosity He gave to me;
     And according to His majestic beauty He made me.

8   I put on incorruption[c] through His name;
     And I stripped off corruption by His grace.

9   Death has been destroyed before my face;
     And Sheol has been vanquished by my word.

10   Since eternal life has arisen in the Lord's land,

---

a. Compare *Ode* 15:1–2 with 1QH[a] 4.5–6 and 9.27.
b. Literally "to delight oneself," "enjoy to the full," "live luxuriously."
c. Or "immortality." Cf. 1 Corinthians 15:54–55.

And become known[d] to His faithful ones,
And been given without limit to all that trust in Him.

Hallelujah.

---

d. Or "been declared."

MY WORK IS THE LORD'S PSALM

1 As the work of the plowman is the plowshare,
   And the work of the helmsman is the steering of the
      ship,
   So my work is the psalm of the Lord in His praises.

2 In His praises are my art and my service,
   Because His love has nourished my heart,
   And His fruits He poured unto my lips.[a]

3 For my love is the Lord;
   Hence I shall sing to Him.

4 For I am strengthened in His praises.
   And I have faith in Him.

5 I shall open my mouth,
   And His spirit shall speak through me
   The glorious praise of the Lord and His beauty,

6 The work of His hands,
   And the service of His fingers;

7 For the multitude of His mercies,
   And the strength of His word.[b]

8 For the word of the Lord investigates the invisible,
   And perceives His thought.

9 For the eye sees His works;
   And the ear hears His thought.

a. Compare *Ode* 16:1–2 with Psalm 45:1.

b. In verses 7, 8, 14, and 19, "word" could be capitalized. See *Ode* 7 note e. Compare Genesis 1:1—2:4a; Prayer of Manasseh 3; and also John 1:1–3; *Jubilees* 12:4.

He expanded the
heavens; and He
set the stars.

10   It is He who spread out the earth;[c]
     And placed the waters in the sea.

11   He expanded the heavens;
     And He set the stars.

12   And He set the creation and aroused it;
     Then He rested from His works.[d]

13   And created things run according to their courses;[e]
     And work their works.
     And they are not able to cease and be idle.[f]

14   And the hosts are subject
     To His word.[g]

15   The reservoir of light is the sun;
     And the reservoir of darkness is the night.

16   For He made the sun for the day so that it will be light;
     But night brings darkness over the face of the earth.

17   And (by) their acceptance one from another[h]
     They complete God's beauty.[i]

18   And there is nothing outside of the Lord,
     Because He was before anything came to be.[j]

---

    c. Or "He who made the earth broad . . ." If "Word" (16:7) is the agent of creation in *Ode* 16, cf. John 1:1–18.

    d. Recall Genesis 2:2.

    e. Literally "they run according to their runnings."

    f. Parallels to this concept are abundant; cf. *1 Enoch* 2:1—5:2; 69:20–21; *Psalms of Solomon* 18:12–14; *2 Baruch* 48:9; Sirach 16:26–28.

    g. See the note b to *Ode* 16:7.

    h. Cf. Psalm 19:1.

    i. Cf. *1 Enoch* 69:20; 78:10.

    j. Cf. John 1:1–3; 8:58.

19 And the worlds are by His word,[k]
   And by the thought of His heart.

20 Praise and honor
   To His name.

   Hallelujah.

---

k. See note b to *Ode* 16:7.

MY WREATHED-CROWN IS LIVING

1   Then I was crowned by my God,
     And my wreathed-crown is living.

2   And I was justified by my Lord,
     For my salvation is incorruptible.

3   I have been released from vanities;
     And I am not condemned.

4   My chains were cut off by His hands.
     I received the face and form of a new person;
     And I walked in Him and was saved.

5   And the thought of truth led me;
     And I went after it and did not err.

(Christ Speaks)[a]

6   And all who saw Me were amazed;
     And I seemed to them like a stranger.

7   And He who knew and exalted Me
     Is the Most High in all His perfection.

8   And He glorified Me[b] by His kindness,
     And raised My understanding to truth's height.

9   And from there He gave Me the way of His paths.
     And I opened the doors that were closed.[c]

a. See note d to *Ode* 8.

b. N: "and He is glorified."

c. The passage may refer to those bound by sin on earth. For the idea of *descensus ad inferos* (descent into the nether regions), see *Ode* 24:5, and esp. 42:10–20. Also, see 1 Peter 3:19; John 10:7–10; Revelation 3:7–8.

I was crowned by
my God

10   And I shattered the bars of iron,
      For My own iron(s) had grown hot and melted before
           Me.

11   And nothing appeared closed to Me,[d]
      Because I was the opening of everything.

12   And I went towards all My bondsmen in order to
           loose them,
      That I might not abandon anyone bound or binding.

13   And I gave My knowledge generously,
      And My resurrection[e] through My love.

14   And I sowed My fruits in hearts,
      And transformed them through Myself.

15   Then they received My blessing and lived.
      And they were gathered to Me and were saved,

16   Because they became My members.[f]
      And I was their head.[g]

      (Doxology)[h]

17   Glory to You, our Head,
      O Lord Messiah.

      Hallelujah.

---

d. Cf. John 10:7–10.

e. Literally "My prayer"; *b'wt'* seems to have obtained the meaning "resurrection"; cf. my edition of the *Odes*, p. 77 n. 17.

f. Cf. Romans 12:4–5.

g. Cf. Colossians 1:15–20; John 15.

h. I add this clarifying notation.

Do not withhold
Your perfection from
me

ODE 18

THE LOVE OF THE MOST HIGH

1   My heart was raised and enriched in the love of the
       Most High,
     So that I might praise Him with my name.

2   My members were strengthened,
     That they may not fall from His power.

3   Infirmities fled[a] from my body.
     And it stood[b] firm for the Lord by His will,
     Because His kingdom is firm.[c]

4   O Lord, for the sake of those who are in need,
     Do not dismiss[d] Your word from me.[e]

5   For the sake of their works,
     Do not withhold Your perfection from me.

6   Let not light be conquered by darkness,
     Nor let truth flee from falsehood.[f]

7   Let Your right hand set our salvation to victory.
     And let it receive from every region;
     And preserve (it) on the side of everyone who is
       besieged by evils.

a. H: "they forsook."
b. N: "and they stood."
c. Or "solid," "true," "lasting."
d. H: "do not loose."
e. "Word" could be capitalized; see note e to *Ode* 7:7.
   f. Compare the light-darkness paradigm in the Qumran Scrolls and
John (esp. John 1:5).

8   You are my God, falsehood and death are not in Your
       mouth;
    Only perfection is Your will.

9   And vanity You did not know;
    Because it did not know You.

10   And You did not know error;
    Because it did not know You.

11   And ignorance appeared like dust,
    And like the foam of the sea.

12   And vain people thought that it was great.
    And they became like its form and were impoverished.

13   But the knowledgeable[g] understood and
       contemplated.
    And they were not polluted by their thoughts,

14   Because they were in the mind of the Most High.
    And they mocked those who were walking in error.[h]

15   Then they spoke the truth,
    From the breath that the Most High breathed into
       them.

16   Praise and great honor
    To His name.

    Hallelujah.

g. Lit. "those who knew."

h. Compare this thought with 1QS 3.21; and 4.11–12; as well as John
8:12; and 12:35.

THE CUP OF MILK

1   The cup of milk was offered to me.[a]
And I drank it in the sweetness of the Lord's kindness.

2   The Son is the cup.[b]
And the Father is He who was milked.
And the Holy Spirit is She who milked Him,

3   Because His breasts were full;
And it was undesirable that His milk should be
    released without purpose.

4   The Holy Spirit opened Her bosom,
And mixed the milk of the two breasts of the Father.

5   Then She gave the mixture to the generation[c] without
    their knowing.
And those who have received (it)[d] are in the
    perfection of the right hand.

6   The womb of the Virgin took (it).
And she received conception and gave birth;

7   So the Virgin became a mother
With great mercies.

8   And she labored and bore the Son but without pain,[e]
Because it did not occur without purpose.

a. Cf. 1 Peter 2:3. This *Ode* appears to have echoes of the Eucharist [celebration of the Last Supper].

b. Cf. *Gospel of Truth* 24:9–14.

c. Or "world."

d. See note d to *Ode* 6:8.

e. Cf. *Ascension of Isaiah* 11:2–15.

9   And she did not seek a midwife,
Because He allowed her to give life.

10   She bore with desire as a strong man.
And she bore according to the manifestation;[f]
And she possessed with great power.[g]

11   And she loved with salvation.
And she guarded with kindness.
And she declared[h] with greatness.

Hallelujah.

---

f. Or "example," "demonstration." See Luke 1:26–38.

g. Or "And She acquired according to the Great Power"; if so cf. Mark 14:62; Acts 8:10.

h. Or "manifested"; cf. *Ode* 19:10.

The cup of milk
was offered to me.
And I drank it, in
the sweetness of the
Lord's kindness.

A WREATHED-CROWN
FROM HIS TREE

1   I am a priest of the Lord.
    And to Him I serve as a priest.

2   And to Him I offer the offering of His thought.

3   For His thought is not like the world,
    Nor like the flesh,
    Nor like those who serve[a] according to the flesh.

4   The offering of the Lord is righteousness,
    And purity of heart and lips.

5   Offer your[b] inward being faultlessly.
    And do not let your compassion oppress compassion.
    And you (you especially) do not oppress anyone.[c]

6   You should not purchase a foreigner because he is like
        yourself,[d]
    Nor seek to deceive your neighbor,
    Nor deprive him of the covering for his nakedness.[e]

7   But put on the grace of the Lord generously.
    And come into His Paradise.[f]
    And make for yourself a wreathed-crown from His
        tree.

---

a. Or "worship."
b. N: "my inward being."
c. Or "And do not let your soul oppress a soul." Cf. Exodus 22:21.
d. Or "like your (own) soul." Cf. Sirach 33:30–31.
e. Cf. Exodus 22:26–27.
f. Cf. Revelation 2:7.

You will be anointed
in truth with the
praise of His
holiness

8   Then put (it)^g on your head and be refreshed;
      And recline upon His serenity.

9   For His glory will go before you.
      And you will receive of His kindness and of His
        grace.^h
      And you will be anointed in truth with the praise of
        His holiness.

10   Praise and honor
      To His name.

      Hallelujah.

g. See note d to *Ode* 6:8.

h. Or "and of His goodness." N: "of His goodness" (a slightly different noun; cf. my edition of the *Odes*, p. 87 n. 6). Cf. Isaiah 58:8.

ODE 21

THE LORD'S GRACE

1   I raised my arms[a] on high
      On account of the Lord's grace.

2   Because He cast off my chains from me,
      And my Helper raised me according to His grace and
        His salvation.[b]

3   And I stripped off darkness.
      And I put on light.[c]

4   And even I acquired members.
      In them there was no[d] sickness
      Or affliction or suffering.

5   And abundantly helpful to me was the Lord's thought,
      And His incorruptible[e] fellowship.

6   And I was lifted up in the light,
      And I passed before His face.

7   And I was constantly near Him,
      While praising and confessing Him.

8   He caused my heart to overflow.[f]
      And it was found in my mouth.
      And it sprang forth unto my lips.

a. N: "arm."
b. See note a to *Odes* 7:3.
c. Cf. Baruch 4:20; 5:1–2. Also see *Ode* 11:11 and note.
d. H omits.
e. Or "everlasting," "immortal."
f. See *Ode* 8:1, but another verb is chosen, and it also means "abound."

9   Then upon my face increased
     The exultation of the Lord and His praise.[g]

Hallelujah.

g. N: "in His praise."

I stripped off
darkness and I put
on light

In every place
Your name
surrounded Me

ODE 22

THE HOLY ONES'
DWELLING PLACE

(Christ Speaks)[a]

1   He who caused Me to descend from on high,
       And to ascend from the regions below;[b]

2   And He who gathers what is in the middle,
       And throws them[c] to Me;[d]

3   He who scattered My enemies,
       And My adversaries;

4   He who gave Me authority over chains,
       So that I might loosen them.

5   He who overthrew by My hands the dragon with
       seven heads,[e]
       And placed Me[f] at his roots[g] that I might destroy his
       seed.

6   You were there and helped Me;
       And in every place Your name surrounded[h] Me.

---

a. See note e to *Ode* 8.

b. C: "from the regions that are in the deep below."

c. H omits.

d. C: "He who took those who were in the middle, / And has taught Me concerning them."

e. Cf. Revelation 12:3.

f. Following C; both H and N: "and You set Me."

g. N: "His root."

h. H: "A blessing"; C agrees with N.

7   Your right hand destroyed the evil poison.[i]
    And Your hand leveled the way for those who believe
        in You.

8   And it chose them[j] from the graves,
    And separated them[k] from the dead ones.

9   It took dead bones[l]
    And covered them with flesh.

10 But they were motionless,
    So it gave (them) energy[m] for life.

11 Incorruptible was Your way and Your face.
    You allowed your world to become corruptible,
    That everything might be broken and then renewed.

12 And the foundation of everything is Your rock.[n]
    And upon it You built Your kingdom.
    And it[o] became the dwelling place of the holy ones.[p]

    Hallelujah.

i. Cf. 1QH^a 5.10, 27; and CD 8.9; 19.22.
j. C: "You redeemed them from . . ."
k. C: "You removed them from . . ."
l. Cf. Ezekiel 37:1–6.
m. H: "help," "assistance." C agrees with N.
n. C: "Your light." Cf. 1QH^a 6.25–26; and esp. Matthew 16:18.
o. H: "and You became."
p. Or, "the Holy Ones;" Cf. 1QS 8.8; 1QM 12.2; 1QH^a 12.2; 1QSb 4.25.

ODE 23

JOY IS FOR THE ELECT ONES

1   Joy is for the holy ones.[a]
And who will put it on but they alone?

2   Grace is for the elect ones.
And who will receive it, but they who trusted in it
    from the beginning?

3   Love is for the elect ones.
And who will put it on, but they who possessed it
    from the beginning?

4   Walk in the knowledge of the Lord.[b]
And you will know the Lord's grace[c] generously,
Both for His exultation and for the perfection of His
    knowledge.

5   And His thought was like a letter.[d]
And His will descended from on high.

6   And it was sent from a bow like an arrow
That has been forcefully shot.

7   And many hands rushed to the letter,
In order to catch (it),[e] and take, and read it.

8   But it escaped from their fingers.
And they were afraid of it and of the seal that was
    upon it.

---

a. Perhaps "Holy Ones;" cf. Wisdom of Solomon 3:9; 4:15.
b. H: "Most High."
c. H omits "And you will know the grace of the Lord."
d. Cf. Zechariah 5:1–2; and esp. the *Hymn of the Pearl* 40–55.
e. Cf. note d to *Ode* 6:8.

9   Because they were not allowed to loosen its seal,
     For the power that was over the seal was better than
          they.

10   But those who saw the letter went after it,
     That they might know where it would land,
     And who should read it,
     And who should hear it.

11   But a wheel received it.
     And it (the letter) came over it.

12   And with it was a sign,
     Of the kingdom and of providence.

13   And everything that was disturbing the wheel,
     It mowed and cut down.

14   And it restrained a multitude of adversaries.
     And it bridged[f] rivers.

15   And it crossed over (and) uprooted many forests,[g]
     And made a wide way.[h]

16   The head went down to the feet,
     Because unto the feet ran the wheel,
     And whatever had come upon it.

17   The letter was one of command,
     And hence all regions were gathered together.

18   And there appeared at its head, the Head who was
          revealed,
     Even the Son of Truth from the Most High Father.

f. Lit. "covered with earth."
g. N: "peoples," or "Gentiles."
h. Or "an open way."

Joy is for the
holy ones.
And who will put
it on but they
alone?

19   And He inherited and possessed everything,
     And then the scheming^i of the many ceased.

20   Then all the seducers became headstrong and fled.
     And the persecutors became extinct and were blotted
        out.^j

21   And the letter became a large volume,
     Which was entirely written by the finger of God.

22   And the name of the Father was upon it,
     And of the Son and of the Holy Spirit,
     To rule forever and ever.

     Hallelujah.

---

i. Or "thought."
j. H: "and were angry."

OUR LORD MESSIAH

1   The dove fluttered over the head of our Lord Messiah,[a]
Because He was her Head.

2   And she sang over Him.
And her voice was heard.[b]

3   Then the inhabitants were afraid;
And the foreigners were disturbed.

4   The bird began to fly,[c]
And every creeping thing died in its hole.

5   And the chasms were opened and closed;
And they were seeking the Lord as those who are
    about to give birth.[d]

6   But He was not given to them for nourishment,
Because He did not belong to them.

7   But the chasms were submerged in the submersion of
    the Lord.
And they perished in that thought in which they
    remained from the beginning,

8   For they labored from the beginning.
And the end of their labor was life.

---

a. H: "The dove fluttered over the Messiah . . ."

b. *Ode* 24:1–2 is an allusion to Jesus' baptism.

c. N: "she flew."

d. Cf. 1QH[a] 3.16–18. The *descensus ad inferos* ("descent into hell") is portrayed in *Ode* 42:11–20; cf. *Ode* 17:6–16 and notes to those verses.

The dove fluttered
over the head of our
Lord Messiah

9   And all of them who were lacking perished,
     Because they were not able to express the word so that
          they might remain.

10   And the Lord destroyed the thoughts,
     Of all those who did not have the truth with them.

11   For they were lacking in wisdom,
     They who exalted themselves in their mind.[e]

12   So they were rejected,
     Because the truth was not with them.

13   For the Lord declared[f] His way.
     And He spread out His grace.

14   And those who recognized it
     Knew His holiness.

     Hallelujah.

e. Or "heart."
f. Or "revealed."

Your right hand

raised me

ODE 25

MY HELPER

1   I was rescued from my chains;[a]
    And I fled unto You, O my God.[b]

2   Because You are the right hand of salvation,[c]
    And my Helper.

3   You have restrained those who rise up against me,
    And they did not appear again.[d]

4   Because Your face was with me,
    Which saved me by Your grace.[e]

5   But I was despised and rejected in the eyes of many,
    And I was in their eyes like lead.

6   And I acquired strength from You,
    And help.

7   A lamp you set for me both on my right and on my
        left,
    So that there might not be in me anything that is not
        light.

8   And I was covered with the covering of Your spirit,[f]
    And I removed from me my garments of skin.[g]

a. C: "the bonds."
b. C: "O Lord."
c. C: "For You became for me a right hand by which You saved me."
d. H: "I shall not see Him." C: "They have not shown themselves."
e. Cf. Genesis 32:30.
f. C: "of Your mercy."
g. H: "the garments of skins." Cf. *Gospel of Truth* 20:30–34; and 1QS
4.7–8.

75

9   Because Your right hand raised me,
     And caused sickness to pass from me.

10   And I became mighty in Your truth,[h]
     And holy in Your righteousness.

11   And all my adversaries[i] were afraid of me,[j]
     And I became the Lord's by the name of the Lord.[k]

12   And I was justified by His kindness,[l]
     And His rest[m] is for ever and ever.

     Hallelujah.

h. H: "in truth"; C agrees with N.

i. Literally "all those who are against me."

j. C: "my enemies became far from me."

k. C omits this line. Without this line one would imagine that the thoughts are attributed to Christ (*ex ore Christi*). Perhaps the Odist is imagining for himself the thoughts he attributes to Christ in *Ode* 28:9–20.

l. Or "gentleness," "sweetness," "gladness." C: "Your gentleness."

m. C: "Your rest." Cf. Hebrews 4:1.

THE ODISTS STAND IN SERENITY

1   I poured out praise to the Lord,
     Because I am His own.[a]

2   And I will recite His holy ode,
     Because my heart is with Him.

3   For His harp is in my hand;
     And the odes of His rest shall not be silent.

4   I will call unto Him with all my heart,[b]
     I will praise and exalt Him with all my members.

5   For from the East and unto the West
     Is His praise.

6   Also from the South and unto the North
     Is His thanksgiving.[c]

7   Even from the peak of the summits and unto their end
     Is His perfection.

8   Who can write the odes of the Lord;[d]
     Or who can read them?[e]

9   Or who can train himself for life,
     So that he will be (truly) saved?

10   Or who can press upon the Most High,
     So that He would recite from his mouth?

a. Cf. Psalm 45:1.
b. Cf. Psalm 119:145.
c. Or "confession," "praise," "acknowledgement."
d. Cf. Psalm 151:4 [5ApocSyrPss].
e. Cf. Ecclesiastes 7:24; 2 *Baruch* 14:8–9; and 75:1–5.

Who can interpret
the wonders of the
Lord?

11   Who can interpret the wonders of the Lord?[f]
     Though he who interprets should perish,[g]
     Yet that which was interpreted will remain.

12   For it suffices to perceive and be satisfied,
     For the Odists stand in serenity;

13   Like a river which has an increasingly gushing spring,
     And flows to the relief of them that seek it.

     Hallelujah.

f. Cf. Psalm 106:2.
g. Or "should be destroyed."

I extended my hands

And hallowed my

Lord

ODE 27

THE UPRIGHT CROSS

1   I extended my hands[a]
    And hallowed my Lord;

2   For the expansion of my hands
    Is His sign.[b]

3   And my extension
    Is the upright cross.

    Hallelujah.

a. See *Ode* 42:1–2.
b. N: "it was hindered."

As the wings of
doves over their
nestlings . . . so
also are the wings
of the Spirit over
my heart

IMMORTAL LIFE EMBRACED ME

1   As the wings of doves over their nestlings,
        And the mouths of their nestlings toward their
            mouths,
        So also are the wings of the Spirit over my heart.

2   My heart continually refreshes itself and leaps for joy,
        Like the babe who leaps for joy in his mother's womb.[a]

3   I trusted, consequently I was at rest,
        Because trustful is He in whom I trusted.

4   He has greatly blessed me;
        And my head is with Him.

5   And the dagger shall not divide me from Him,[b]
        Nor the sword.[c]

6   Because I am ready[d] before destruction comes;
        And I have been placed in His incorruptible arms.[e]

7   And immortal life embraced me,[f]
        And kissed me.

8   And from that (life) is the Spirit that is within me.
        And it cannot die because She is life.

a. Cf. Psalm 22:9–10; and Luke 1:44.
b. Cf. Romans 8:35.
c. Cf. Psalm 22:20.
d. H: "I made ready."
e. Or "wing," "bosom," "side."
f. H: "and they went out."

(Christ Speaks)^g

9   Those who saw Me were amazed,
Because I was persecuted.

10   And they thought that I had been swallowed up,
Because I appeared to them as one of the lost.

11   But My defamation
Became My salvation.

12   And I became their abomination,
Because there was no jealousy[h] in Me.

13   Because I continually did good to every man,
I was hated.

14   And they surrounded me like mad dogs,[i]
Those who in stupidity[j] attack their masters,

15   Because their mind is depraved,
And their sense is perverted.

16   But I was carrying water in My right hand.
And their bitterness I endured[k] by My sweetness.

17   And I did not perish, because I was not their brother,
Nor was My birth like theirs.[l]

---

g. See note d to *Ode* 8:8. The Odist is empathetic to Jesus' passion and crucifixion.

h. Or "zeal."

i. Note the influence of Psalm 22:16 here and in the Evangelists' narrative of Jesus' crucifixion.

j. H: "because they do not know."

k. N: "I disregarded."

l. N: "nor did they acknowledge My birth." Cf. *Ode* 19.

18   And they sought My death but were unsuccessful,[m]
     Because I was older than their memory;[n]
     And in vain did they cast lots[o] against Me.[p]

19   And those who were after Me[q]
     Sought in vain to destroy the memorial of Him who
       was before them.[r]

20   Because the mind of the Most High cannot be
       prepossessed;[s]
     And His heart is superior to all wisdom.

     Hallelujah.

He declared to me
His sign and He
led me by His
light

THE LORD IS MY HOPE

1   The Lord is my hope.[a]
    I shall not be confused by Him.

2   For according to His praise He made me;
    And according to His grace[b] thus He gave to me.

3   And according to His mercies He raised me up;
    And according to His great honor He lifted me up.

4   And He caused me to ascend from the depths of
        Sheol,
    And from the mouth of Death He drew me.

5   And I humbled my enemies;
    And He justified me by His grace.

6   For I believed in the Lord's Messiah.
    And I considered that He is the Lord.

7   And He declared to me[c] His sign.
    And He led me by His light.[d]

8   And He gave me the scepter of His power,[e]
    That I might subdue the thoughts of the Gentiles,
    And humble the strength of the mighty,

a. Cf. Psalms 31:1 and 71:1.
b. Or "goodness," "kindness."
c. H: "to him."
d. Perhaps "light" should be capitalized as in *Odes* 10:1 and 36:3.
e. Cf. Psalm 110:2.

9   To make war by His word,[f]
      And to take victory by His power.[g]

10   And the Lord overthrew my enemy[h] by His word;[i]
      And he became like the dust that a breeze carries off.[j]

11   And I gave praise to the Most High,
      Because He has magnified His servant
      And the son of His maidservant.[k]

Hallelujah.

f. Or "Word"; see note e to *Ode* 7:7.
g. Cf. 1QM 11.4.
h. H: "my enemies."
i. Or "Word"; see note f above.
j. Cf. Psalm 1:4.
k. See Psalm 116:16; cf. Luke 1:38.

ODE 30

THE LORD'S LIVING SPRING

1 Fill for yourselves water from the living spring[a]
      of the Lord,[b]
   Because it has been opened for you.[c]

2 And come all you thirsty and take a drink,[d]
   And rest beside the spring[e] of the Lord

3 Because it is pleasing and sparkling,
   And perpetually pleases the soul.[f]

4 For more refreshing is its water than honey,[g]
   And the honeycomb of bees cannot be compared
      with it;

5 Because it flowed from the lips of the Lord,
   And it assumed a name from the heart of the Lord.[h]

6 And it came boundless and invisible,
   And until it was set in the middle they knew it not.[i]

a. Or "fountain;" cf. 1QH[a] 8.14.
b. Cf. *1 Enoch* 48:1–10.
c. Cf. Revelation 21:6.
d. Cf. Revelation 22:17.
e. Or "fountain."
f. Or "the breath of life."
g. Cf. Psalm 19:10; and Sirach 24:20.
h. "It" denotes "the water" that flows from the Lord's fountain. Perhaps the Odist is imagining how "water" is associated with naming. Most likely, the Odist is drawing a connection between water and naming at baptism.
i. Or "And until He was set in the middle they knew Him not." Cf. John 1:26.

7   Blessed are they who have drunk from it,
And have rested by it.

Hallelujah.

More refreshing
is its water than
honey

ODE 31

IMMORTAL LIFE

1 Chasms vanished before the Lord,[a]
   And darkness was destroyed by His appearance.[b]

2 Error erred and perished on account of Him;
   And Contempt received[c] no path,
   For it was submerged by the truth of the Lord.

3 He opened His mouth and spoke grace and joy,
   And received a new song[d] for His name.

4 Then He raised His voice towards the Most High,
   And offered to Him those that had become sons
       through Him.[e]

5 And His face was justified,
   Because thus His Holy Father had given to Him.

   (Christ Speaks)[f]

6 Come forth, you who have been afflicted,
   And receive joy.

7 And possess yourselves through grace,
   And take unto you immortal life.

8 And they condemned Me when I stood up,
   Me who had not been condemned.[g]

a. The Odist seems to be referring to Jesus Christ as "Lord."
b. Note the closeness to Johannine Christology.
c. H: "I gave her . . ." or "she was given it . . ."
d. Or "praise."
e. Cf. John 17:1–9.
f. See note d to *Ode* 8:8.
g. Or "who had been found not guilty."

Come forth,
you who have been
afflicted, and receive

joy

9   Then they divided[h] My spoil,
Though nothing was owed them.

10   But I endured and held My peace and was silent,
That I might not be disturbed by them.

11   But I stood undisturbed like a solid rock,
Which is continuously pounded by columns of waves
and endures.[i]

12   And I bore their bitterness because of humility;
That I might save My nation and instruct it.

13   And that I might not nullify the promises to the
patriarchs,[j]
To whom I was promised for the salvation of their
offspring.

Hallelujah.

---

h. N: "and he divided;" cf. Psalm 22:18 and its influence on the Evangelists' narration of Jesus' passion and crucifixion.

i. H: "pounded by waves and endures."

j. Cf. Romans 15:8.

JOY FROM THE HEART

1   To the blessed ones joy is from their heart,
     And light from Him who dwells in them;

2   And the Word from the truth
     Who is self-originative,[a]

3   Because He has been strengthened
        by the holy power of the Most High;
     And He is unshaken for ever and ever.

     Hallelujah.

---

a. Literally "He who is from Himself"; N omits "from." Cf. John 1:1–18.

To the blessed ones
joy is from their
heart,
And light from
Him who dwells in
them

THE PERFECT VIRGIN IS JUDGE

1   But again Grace was swift and repudiated the
        Corruptor,[a]
    And descended upon him to renounce him.

2   And he caused utter[b] destruction before him;
    And he corrupted all his construction.[c]

3   And he stood on a summit's peak and cried aloud
    From one end of the earth to the other.

4   Then he drew to him all those who obeyed him,
    For[d] he did not appear as the Evil One.

5   However the perfect Virgin[e] stood,
    Who was preaching and summoning[f] and saying:

6   "O you sons of men, return,
    And you their daughters, come.

7   And abandon the ways of that Corruptor,[g]
    And approach Me.

8   And I will enter into you,
    And bring you forth from destruction.
    And make you wise in the ways of truth.

---

a. Or "dismissed the Destroyer;" cf. Revelation 9:11.

b. Literally "he has destroyed the destruction."

c. Or "composition," "work."

d. Or "and," "then," "yet."

e. Cf. the fourth vision of the *Shepherd of Hermas*; contrast Proverbs 1:20–21; 8:1–4.

f. N: "and shouting."

g. Cf. 1QM 14.10.

9   Be not corrupted,
    Nor perish.

10 Hearken unto Me and be saved,
    For I am proclaiming unto you the grace of God.

11 And through Me you will be saved and become
        blessed.
    I am your judge.[h]

12 And they who have put Me on will not be rejected,[i]
    But they will possess incorruption in the new world.

13 My elect ones have walked with Me.
    And I shall allow those who seek Me to know My
        ways.
    And I shall promise them My name."

    Hallelujah.

---

h. Contrast *1 Enoch* and the Gospels in which the Son of Man is judge.

i. Or "will not be rejected . . ."

I am proclaiming

unto you

the grace of God

THE SIMPLE HEART

1   There is no hard way where there is a simple heart,
     Nor barrier for upright thoughts,

2   Nor whirlwind in the depth
     Of the enlightened thought.

3   Where one is surrounded entirely[a] (by) pleasing
          country,
     There is nothing divided in him.

4   The likeness[b] of that which is below[c]
     Is that which is above.

5   For everything is from above,
     And from below there is nothing,
     But it is considered[d] so by those lacking
          understanding.[e]

6   Grace has been revealed for your salvation.
     Believe, and live, and be saved.

     Hallelujah.

---

a. Or "on every side."
b. Or "form."
c. Cf. *Ascension of Isaiah* 7:10.
d. Or "believed."
e. Or "knowledge." Recall the use of irony in the Gospel of John and the paradigmatic meaning of "above" and "below."

Believe, and live,

and be saved

ODE 35

THE LORD'S DEW

1   The Lord's gentle shower overshadowed me with
    serenity,[a]
    And it caused a cloud of peace to remain over my
    head,

2   That it might guard me at all times.
    And it became salvation[b] for me.

3   Everyone was disturbed and afraid,
    And there flowed from them smoke and judgment.

4   But I was tranquil[c] in the Lord's legion;
    More than a shade[d] was He to me, and more than
    foundation.

5   And I was carried like a babe by its mother;
    And He gave me milk, the dew of the Lord.[e]

6   And I grew strong in His favor.
    And I rested in His perfection.

7   And I extended my hands in the ascent of my soul.[f]
    And I directed myself near[g] the Most High.
    And I was saved near[h] Him.

    Hallelujah.

a. H: "with rest."
b. H: "in salvation."
c. Or "I was silent."
d. N: "dew."
e. Cf. *Ode* 19. *4 Ezra* 8:10 refers to milk as "the fruit of the breasts." *1 Enoch* 39:5 mentions "mercy like dew upon the earth."
f. Cf. Tertullian *De oratione* 14.
g. Or "towards," "with."
h. Or "towards," "with."

I grew strong in
His favor,
and I rested in His
perfection

I rested on the
Spirit of the Lord,
and she raised me up
to heaven

ODE 36

THE LORD'S HIGH PLACE

1   I rested on the Spirit of the Lord.
      And She raised me up to heaven.[a]

2   And She caused me to stand on my feet in the Lord's
          high place,
      Before His perfection and His glory,
      Where I continued praising (Him)[b] by the
          composition of His odes.

(Christ Speaks)[c]

3   (The Spirit) brought Me forth before the Lord's face.[d]
      And because[e] I was the Son of Man,
      I was named the Light, the Son of God,

4   Because I was the most praised among the praised,[f]
      And the greatest among the great ones.[g]

5   For according to the greatness of the Most High, so
          She made Me;
      And according to His newness He renewed Me.

6   And He anointed Me with His perfection;
      And I became one of those who are near Him.

---

a. Or "height"; H: "on high."

b. See note d to *Ode* 6:8.

c. See note d to *Ode* 8:8.

d. Cf. *1 Enoch* 48:2–10.

e. Or "when," "after," "although," "while."

f. Or "the most glorified among the glorious ones . . ." H: "the most glorified among those who glorify . . ." Cf. Hebrews 1:3–4.

g. Cf. *2 Enoch* 22:10 (13); 3 Maccabees 2:2, "holy among the holy ones"; and *Acts of Thomas* 101–105.

7   And My mouth was opened like a cloud of dew,
     And My heart gushed forth[h] (like)[i] a gusher of
        righteousness.

8   And My approach was in peace,
     And I was established in the spirit of providence.

     Hallelujah.

---

h. Lit. "to vomit," "reject."
i. This adverb is sometimes assumed in Semitic texts.

THE LIPS OF MY HEART

1   I extended my hands toward the Lord,[a]
      And towards the Most High I raised my voice.

2   And I spoke with the lips of my heart,[b]
      And He heard me when my voice reached Him.

3   His Word came towards me,[c]
      That which gave me the fruits of my labors;

4   And gave me rest
      By the grace of the Lord.

Hallelujah.

a. H: "my Lord."
b. Cf. *Psalms of Solomon* 15:5(3); and Prayer of Manasseh 11.
c. See note e to *Ode* 7:7.

His Word came

towards me

ODE 38

THE LIGHT OF TRUTH

1   I went up into the light of Truth as into a chariot,
     And Truth led me and allowed me to proceed.[a]

2   And He allowed me to pass over chasms and gulfs.[b]
     And He saved me from cliffs and valleys.[c]

3   And He became for me a haven of salvation.
     And He set me on the place[d] of immortal life.

4   And He went with me and allowed me to rest and did
          not allow me to err,
     Because He was and is the Truth.

5   And there was no danger for me because I constantly
          walked with Him.
     And I did not err in anything because I obeyed Him.

6   For Error fled from Him.
     And It never met Him.

7   But Truth was proceeding on the upright way,
     And whatever I did not understand He declared to
          me:

8   All the drugs of Error,
     And pains of death that are considered[e] sweetness.

a. Cf. Psalm 43:3.
b. N: "over empty chasms and gulfs."
c. Lit. "ground liable to be flooded."
d. Lit. "step," "degree," "condition." H: "arms."
e. H: "they who think."

I went up into the light of Truth as into a chariot

9   And the corrupting of the Corruptor,[f]
    I saw when the Bride who was corrupting[g] was
       adorned,
    And the Bridegroom who corrupts and is corrupted.

10   And I asked the Truth, "Who are these?"
    And He said to me: "This is the Deceiver[h] and the
       Error."[i]

11   And They imitate the Beloved and His Bride,[j]
    And They cause the world to err and corrupt it.

12   And They invite many to the wedding feast,[k]
    And caused them to drink the wine of their
       intoxication;[l]

13   So They cause them to vomit up their wisdom and
       their knowledge,
    And make them senseless.[m]

14   Then They abandon them;
    And so they stumble about like mad[n] and corrupted
       men.

15   There is no understanding[o] in them,
    Therefore they do seek it.

f. Cf. Revelation 9:11.

g. H: "who was being corrupted."

h. Or "Imposter," "Seducer." In *Testament of Job* 3:3 the devil is one
who deceives; cf. *Apocalypse of Moses* 39:2.

i. Or "one who is straying."

j. Cf. *Ascension of Isaiah* 4:6.

k. Or "banquet," "marriage."

l. Cf. *Odes* 38:9–12 and 42:8–9 with *Acts of Thomas* 11–16.

m. Literally "no mind," "no sense."

n. H: "Commanders."

o. Literally "a heart."

16 But I have been made wise so as not to fall into the
hands of the deceivers.[p]
And I inwardly rejoiced because Truth had gone with
me.

17 For I was established and lived and was saved.
And my foundations were laid on account of the
Lord's hand,
Because He planted me.[q]

18 For He set the root.
And He watered it, and adapted it, and blessed it.
And its fruits will be forever.

19 It penetrated deeply and sprang up and spread out.[r]
And it was full and enlarged.

20 And the Lord alone was praised,
In His planting[s] and in His cultivation,

21 In His care and in the blessing of His lips,
In the beautiful planting of His right hand,

22 And in the attainment[t] of His planting,
And in the understanding of His mind.

Hallelujah.

---

p. H: "Deceiver."

q. Cf. 1 Corinthians 3:6–10; and *Psalms of Solomon* 14; cf. *Ode* 11; and 1QH[a] 18.

r. H: "it deepened and raised and enriched."

s. Cf. 1QH[a] 6.15; 8.5; 1QS 8.5; 11.8.

t. Or "finding," "discovery," "existence."

ODE 39

THE LORD'S POWER

1   Raging rivers (are like)[a] the power of the Lord;
     They cast headlong those who despise Him.

2   And the (rivers) entangle their paths,
     And obliterate their crossings.[b]

3   And they catch their bodies,
     And corrupt their natures.

4   For they are more swift than lightnings,[c]
     Even more rapid.

5   But those who cross them in faith
     Shall not be disturbed.[d]

6   And those who walk on them faultlessly[e]
     Shall not be shaken.

7   Because the sign on them is the Lord,
     And the sign is the Way for those who cross in the
        name of the Lord.

8   Therefore, put on the name of the Most High and
        know him,
     And you shall cross without danger;[f]
     Because the rivers shall be obedient to you.

a. Semitic languages are frequently cryptic.

b. Or "ways," "passages," "fords."

c. H: "lightning."

d. 2 Ezra 8:50–53 also preserves the claim that the Lord protects his
children during a journey. Cf. Tobit 5:16–22.

e. Cf. *Psalms of Solomon* 6:5.

f. Cf. *Ode* 38:5.

9   The Lord has bridged them by his word,[g]
    And He walked and crossed them on foot.

10 And His footsteps stood firm upon the waters, and
        were not destroyed;
    But they are like a beam[h] (of wood) that is
        constructed[i] on truth.[j]

11 On this side and on that the waves were lifted up,
    But the footsteps of our Lord Messiah stood firm.

12 And they are not blotted out;
    Neither are they destroyed.

13 And the Way has been appointed for those who cross
        over after Him,
    And for those who adhere to the path of His faith;
    And who adore His name.

    Hallelujah.

g. Or "Word"; see note e to *Ode* 7:7.
h. Or "cross."
i. Or "firmly fixed."
j. This verse appears to refer obliquely to the tradition that Jesus walked on water.

Put on the name
of the Most High
and know him

ODE 40

THE LORD'S ODES OF IMMORTALITY

1   As honey drips from the honeycomb of bees,
    And milk flows from the woman who loves her
        infants,[a]
    So also is my hope upon you, O my God.

2   As a spring[b] gushes forth its water,
    So my heart gushes forth the praise of the Lord.
    And my lips bring forth praise to Him.

3   And my tongue becomes sweet by His anthems.
    And my members[c] are anointed by His odes.[d]

4   My[e] face rejoices in His exultation.
    And my spirit exults in His love.
    And my nature shines in Him.

5   And he who is afraid shall trust in Him.
    And salvation will be established in him.[f]

6   And his possession[g] is immortal life.
    And those who receive it are incorruptible.

    Hallelujah.

---

a. Or "her children." See *Ode* 41:1–2.
b. Or "fountain."
c. Lit. "[my] me[mbe]rs." Brackets restore the letters lost.
d. H: "And my tongue by His odes."
e. N omits.
f. Or "And redemption will be assured for him."
g. Or "profit," "gain."

My spirit exults in His love

A great day
has shined upon us

OUR HEARTS MEDITATE
IN HIS LOVE

1   Let all the Lord's babes praise Him.[a]
     And let us[b] receive the truth of His faith.

2   And His children shall be acknowledged[c] by Him;
     Therefore let us sing by His love.

3   We live[d] in the Lord by His grace.
     And life we receive by His Messiah.

4   For a great day has shined upon us.
     And wonderful is He who has given to us[e] of His
          glory.

5   Let us, therefore, all of us agree in the name of the
          Lord.
     And let us honor Him in His goodness.

6   And let our faces shine in His light.
     And let our hearts meditate in His love,
     By night and by day.[f]

7   Let us exult with the exultation of the Lord.

a. Literally: "They will praise the Lord, all of his infants." N: "Let us praise."

b. N: "and let them receive."

c. Or "shall be known . . . "

d. N: "we rejoice."

e. N omits "to us."

f. Cf. Psalm 1:2. This well-known Psalm obviously shaped the Odist's poetry.

(Christ Speaks)[g]

8   All those who see Me will be amazed,
    Because I am from another race.

9   For the Father of Truth remembered Me,
    He who possessed Me from the beginning.[h]

10   For His riches begat Me,
    And the thought of His heart.

(The Odist Speaks)[i]

11   And His Word is with us in all our way,
    The Savior who gives life and does not reject our
       souls.[j]

12   The Man who humbled Himself,
    But was raised because of His own righteousness.[k]

13   The Son of the Most High appeared
    In the perfection of His Father.

14   And light dawned from the Word
    That was before time in Him.[l]

15   The Messiah in truth is one.
    And He was known before the foundations of the
       world,
    That He might give life to persons forever by the truth
       of His name.[m]

g. See note d to *Ode* 8:8.
h. Cf. Proverbs 8:22–23.
i. I add this notation.
j. Cf. John 6:33–37.
k. Cf. Philippians 2:6–9.
l. Cf. John 1:1.
m. Cf. John 17:24.

(Doxology)[n]

16 A new song[o] (is) for the Lord from them that love
Him.

Hallelujah.

n. I add this clarification.
o. Or "praise."

Bring us out from
the chains of
darkness

ODE 42

THE RIGHTEOUS ONE:
OUR SAVIOR

1 I extended my hands and approached my Lord,[a]
  Because the stretching out of my hands is His sign.[b]

2 And my extension is the common[c] cross,[d]
  That was lifted up on the way of the Righteous One.[e]

(Christ Speaks)[f]

3 And I became useless to those[g] who knew Me [not],
  Because I shall hide myself from those who possessed
   Me not.

4 And I will be with those
  Who love Me.

5 All My persecutors are dead;
  But they who trusted in Me sought Me, because I am
   alive.[h]

6 Then I arose and am with them.
  And I will speak by their mouths.

7 For they have rejected those who persecute them.
  And I threw over them the yoke of My love.

---

a. Recall *Ode* 27:1–3.

b. According to this verse, "His sign" is the upright cross. The worshipper assumes this form in praying and singing.

c. Or "simple," "erect," "plain."

d. Or "wood," "tree."

e. Cf. *1 Enoch* 38:2; 53:6.

f. See note d to *Ode* 8:8.

g. H omits the words between "to those" and "from those."

h. Or "pure."

8   Like the arm of the bridegroom over the bride,
    So is My yoke over those who know Me.

9   And as the bridal feast[i] is spread out by the bridal
        pair's home,
    So is My love by those who believe in Me.

10 I was not rejected although I was considered to be so.
    And I did not perish although they thought it of Me.

11 Sheol saw Me and was shattered.[j]
    And Death ejected Me and many with Me.

12 I have been vinegar and bitterness to it.
    And I went down with it as far as its depth.

13 Then the feet and the head it released,
    Because it was[k] not able to endure My face.

14 And I made a congregation of living (people) among
        his dead ones.
    And I spoke with them by living lips,
    In order that My word may not fail.

15 And those who had died ran towards Me.
    And they cried out and said:
    "Son of God, have pity on us.

16 And deal with us according to Your kindness,
    And bring us out from the chains of darkness.

i. Or "bed," "couch," "bridal chamber."
j. Cf. Revelation 20:13–14.
k. H: "they were."

17   And open for us the door[l]
       By which we may proceed to You,[m]
       For we perceive that our death does not approach You.

18   May we also be saved with You,
       Because You are our Savior."

19   Then I heard their voice,
       And placed their faith in My heart.[n]

20   And I placed My name upon their head,
       Because they are free[o] and they are mine.

(Doxology)[p]

Hallelujah.

l. Cf. John 10:7–10.
m. Cf. Revelation 3:7–8.
n. H omits verse 19b.
o. Or "nobles," "princes."
p. I add this notation.

INDEX OF ANCIENT SOURCES